# My Spirit Bubble

## By

## Shirley Bach

Pheonix Publishing,
Rose Cottage,
Doctors Hill,
Bournheath,
Worcs, B61 9JE


Printed and bound in Great Britain by
www.printondemand-worldwide.com (Peterborough)

# Contents

# The Seven Principles
# Of Spiritualism

1.  **The Fatherhood of God.**

2.  **The Brotherhood of Man.**

3.  **The Communion of Spirits and the Ministry of Angels.**

4.  **The Continuous Existence of the Human Soul.**

5.  **Personal Responsibility.**

6.  **Compensation and Retribution Hereafter for all the Good and Evil Deeds done on Earth.**

7.  **Eternal Progress Open to Every Human Soul.**

# Serenity

**God grant me the serenity to accept the things I cannot change, the courage to change what I can, and the wisdom to know the difference.**

# Forward

This book is the story of Shirley's experiences during her last few months of life and hope.  Doubters may dismiss her words as coincidence or conjecture or even wishful thinking.  You will be able to form an opinion, I'm sure, but there is a limit to how many times we can say 'Oh that was just chance' or 'Isn't that strange' and leave it at that.  Many folks get depressed during British Winter months.  This is explained as Seasonal Affective Disorder caused by reduced sunlight and hence vitamin D deficiency. We now accept that there are work environments that make us unhappy.  This discontent, we are told, is not associated with the actual work carried out there but the 'ambience' of our surroundings and that we can improve the situation by altering the layout, colour scheme and seating etc.  Why do we feel more comfortable in the presence of some strangers but not others?  We are told that it's due to appearance, age, sex, reasons for being in their company etc.  We are happy to accept these logical explanations because they fit our way of thinking but we are reticent about accepting other feelings that are not so easily explained.  Surely we have all, at some time, 'sensed' something . It might have been a feeling that someone was standing behind us or perhaps the perception of a friendly 'atmosphere' when walking into a building or a room in that building.  People quite often will say or think the same words at the same time as someone they are talking to.  The subject of the conversation could be completely different from the previous one.  Can we adequately explain this as 'being on the same wavelength' as the other person.  Maybe it's all caused by electro – magnetism or some other convenient phenomena.  Diviners say that they use this, and are frequently employed to locate water pipes or electrical cables by 'dowsing'.  A Spiritualist will tell you that everyone has an Aura around him or her and this is part of our being.  Are we always able to accept that sometimes we are not just a physical person and have a Spiritual, or possibly an 'electro – magnetic' part of us as well?

As humans we find it difficult to accept that our knowledge is limited and we strive to explain natural phenomena scientifically to our satisfaction. Alternatively, we sometimes feel more comfortable if we can dismiss them as weird, a 'con' or imagination etc. I'm sure however that if you go and witness a good Spiritualist medium at work you will find the 'dismissal' option a lot more difficult than you expected. Shirley, like many thousands of others, found that not only were her messages and influences from the Spirit world undeniable but they were also deeply comforting. The warmth, love and comfort found in a Spiritualist Church are special and the background of Shirley's book.

Steve Bach

# Introduction

This is just so daunting. To pick up a pen and notebook and be bold enough to tell yourself "I'm going to write a book." But yesterday I was given a rather large 'shove in this direction'. I really want to achieve this and it's a case of 'now or never' because today my consultant surgeon informed me that my breast cancer has produced three tiny tumours on my liver and the prognosis is not good. The recurrent breast cancer which I was to have removed tomorrow (15th October, 2004) is now not of prime importance to my overall condition so I have decided not to have the operation, not for the time being anyway. Chemotherapy would only ease the situation for a while but at the moment I've decided that's not an option. I am at present half way through a course of 'chemo' and it's made me feel so lousy and low that I don't want to waste any of my life on it now. Maybe, if I become too uncomfortable, I will change my mind who knows. I would have said "yes" if it could cure me but not to prolong my earthly existence. I would sooner 'Pop me Clogs' and go to see what the next place is like.

My last comment gives a clue about what 'makes me tick'. Life to me encompasses far more than earthly life and throughout this book I will endeavour to show you how I've come to this conclusion. I know that this earthly existence is but 'the tip of the iceberg,' the nursery-bed where we are planted out as little seedlings to grow for a while. What my consultant, Mr Purser, has had to tell me today (poor chap) is that I am soon to be re-potted! The words "I know" may strike many as very conceited, but this is what being a Spiritualist does for you, gives you strength and comfort derived from knowledge rather than a reliance on faith. This may be enough for some folk (and I admire these people very much) but it would never have been enough for me. As my surgeon, who would seem to be of the same 'ilk' as myself here, said to me last week "You just can't die, can you Shirley." It's sure nice to feel that someone who is caring for you professionally 'knows where you are coming from.'

Naturally, there are parts of my new situation that are very difficult to cope with. It is the thought of leaving those who we love for which words, here, seem inadequate. I have been with others in the same situation and I realise that others are going to feel worse than I do today. Apart from my husband, Steve and 16-year-old son Paul, I have so many loving and loyal friends who I just love to 'bits'. I am just sitting looking around me at dozens of 'get well' cards and letters which we have draped on strings around our lounge. This love has really overwhelmed me from the start of my illness and it has carried me along throughout. It makes me beg the question 'would I ever have realised how many people care if I hadn't been given this cancer?'

Life really is a strange mixture of good and bad, light and dark, 'ying and yang'. My Mom always said to me that to experience real joy we have to know true sorrow. Everything is bitter sweet, especially so at the moment. Life's ups and downs are like the swing of a pendulum, but as I once read 'Sorrow always carries deeper channels for joy.'

# Preparation via Spirit*

**B**efore I take you back with me to my early life and the events which led me to my present spiritual knowledge, I have to explain my recent links with spirit* and how it's shaping my life in my strange new circumstances.

Anyone who knows me will be aware that the past four years have been pretty disastrous health wise. Beginning in October 2000 when I collapsed with viral pneumonia, then to March 2001 when I ruined a holiday by falling and breaking my wrist on the first day. I spent two days in Taormina Hospital in Sicily (where nobody at all spoke English by the way) before being flown home and straight to the Alexander Hospital at Redditch. I mended well and normal life resumed until May 2002 when I caught chickenpox from I know not where and was extremely poorly. (I had spots in places I didn't even know I had places). I wouldn't wish adult chicken pox on my worst enemy - believe me 45 is not a good age for this childhood disease. Spots finally faded by September and I was feeling my old self again. However, this normal span of life was halted yet again in January this year (2004) when I slipped and broke my ankle. Other people break bones skiing or parachuting but not me; I was simply going over to my neighbour, Gill, for a cuppa and although it was January it wasn't even icy. This last injury was well and truly on the mend when, on Saturday, 29th May, I found a tiny breast lump, which heralded the start of this latest episode. By now, of course, I am viewed by my friends as a 'disaster on legs.'

Being of the opinion that life's events always happen for a reason, I am thinking that spirit* must have been 'toughening me up' for the latest episode. I have certainly got used to hospitals! I know what it's like to be disabled and somewhat reliant on others. I became a real Stirling Moss in the invalid buggy in Sainsbury's, not to mention perfecting the art of one-armed organ playing and then one-legged vacuum cleaning! Joking apart, I have been busy developing coping strategies both physically and mentally. There was a time, believe me, when anything out of the normal routine would really upset the apple cart, but now I say that this is what life's like at the moment, let's just make the best job we can out of it all!

My experience of pneumonia in 2000 was perhaps the most spiritually enlightening of these bad patches. Before I was diagnosed and we simply thought I'd contracted a nasty virus, I wobbled my way downstairs one night, much too restless to sleep. I remember dragging my duvet onto the settee and drinking from a pint glass of cold water trying to satisfy a 'raging' thirst. Little by little my third eye** started to open up. Now I've had the odd glimpse through the third eye before but this was a whole new ball game to me. I saw beautiful colours, trees, lanes and rivers; I felt I could have walked off into this new landscape. The sensation lasted for several minutes and will always remain with me. Some would have clearly categorized this as an 'hallucination' - maybe that's what it was - but for me it was a trip from my normal earthly vibration to a faster spiritual one. I had been given a proper look at what mediums are able to do whenever they 'tune-in.' Several days later I was lying in bed, dosed up with 2000 mg antibiotics for what had now been diagnosed as pneumonia. Now, on the top of my wardrobe there is a vast menagerie of cuddly toy animals and without my glasses these were patches of fuzzy colours blended together in unrecognisable shapes. As I stared up at them a perfect oval shape 'defined' itself amongst the mass and I could see in detail a beautiful little cherub blowing a trumpet. This vision at once lifted my low spirits. Again I must have seen it with my third eye because it was crystal clear amidst the rest of my cloudy vision.

In July this year Steve, Paul and I took a weeklong holiday. We felt this was a well-deserved break as I was recovering from breast surgery and Paul had completed his G.C.S.Es. Still feeling quite tired I would return to the hotel during the afternoon, take a snooze and freshen up.  On one such afternoon I had just laid down and got comfortable when I was given a small snippet of clairvoyance.  In my mind's eye there was a middle-aged man with a high forehead, very short dark curly hair, a cream and green check shirt.  I could even see his complexion was slightly pimply under the skin.  In my mind I asked him who he was and back came the reply "I'm your brother Stephen, Shirley, I've come to say 'Hello'".  Then he went as quickly as he had appeared.  I realised then he looked very much like me, even the same slightly beaky nose and he also had my Dad's features.  My Mother had given birth to two still-born babies prior to having me. The first, a boy, was named Stephen.

16th October 2004. Now we shall move closer to the last fortnight's happenings.  I had discovered a very small lump near the scar from my excision operation on my right breast.  I had this operation at the Alexandra Hospital, Redditch on 22nd June.  Dr Irwin thought it to be scar tissue but sent me to my surgeon, Mr. Purser, for a check-up.  Alarm bells started to ring as Mr. Purser said he thought it wise to take another biopsy.  I had to return to his clinic the following day (7th October) for the result, which was that the cancer had returned, and, most worryingly, in the middle of chemotherapy.  I was given the choice of a second local wide excision or a complete mastectomy.  I opted for the less drastic operation and was booked in for Friday 15th October.  Needless to say I didn't sleep too well on the night of diagnosis.  Steve had been banished to the spare room due to his streaming cold and my being on 'chemo.'  By 1.30am I just couldn't nod off and put on my bedside lamp to read for a while.  Eventually I began to feel sleepy, but decided I might feel more settled if I left the light on.  I lay on my side just getting comfortable when I felt my bed dip down as though someone had sat down and then risen up again.  I turned to see if Steve had seen my light on and come in, but no - the door was still closed, nobody there.  On the following Saturday, at our 'Day of Private Sittings' (Bi-annual event at Bromsgrove Spiritualist Church) I had a reading from a medium called Keith Lloyd who gave me a lovely description of Mom and various family members when he told me  "Your Mom came to sit on your bed the other night because you were so worried and couldn't sleep" adding "You decided to leave your light on like when you were little and didn't like the dark." With evidence like this, I would be really dotty not to believe in the Spirit world, wouldn't I? Keith also told me that soon my husband and son would have proof of the existence of the Spirit World.

On 14<sup>th</sup> October, the day prior to my second 'op,' I was sitting playing the organ in my front room, quite calm, with suitcase packed ready for the morrow. My son Paul had just come home unexpectedly from college and had gone up to the computer room to do some homework. The phone rang and Paul shouted downstairs, "It's Mandy from hospital Mom". I took the call and realised immediately something was very wrong, Mr. Purser wanted to see me straight away. Trying to hang on to my composure I went upstairs to tell Paul that Dad and I had to go to Hospital to 'discuss' my 'op.' As I explained I realised that Paul's attention was elsewhere... "Mom" he said, "You haven't noticed, have you?".... and pointed to the light which was going on and off repeatedly all on it's own accord. Then he said "Mom, the computer screen, look!" - The cursor was vibrating around all on it's own with Paul's hand nowhere near the mouse! His words to me "This is spirit* isn't it?" "Yes" I replied "I suspect it's Nanny Joyce letting us know she's around - are you okay with this Paul?" "Yes" he said, "I'll be okay." As we closed the front door on our way out I heard him shout. "It's okay Mom she's just turned the light off now."

Aside from this very 'hands on' spiritual help, there is another type which arrives more subtly in the form of 'just knowing.' It is a knowing at soul level and has no basis in earthly reality. At times it comes often in the form of a 'gut feeling' about someone or something. It was just a 'just knowing' which turned up a couple of months prior to finding my first breast lump. I remember brushing my shoulder-length hair in front of the bathroom mirror and I just knew it was going to be lost through 'chemo-therapy'. I'm not one given to moan or hypochondria but this drifted into my brain, out of the blue as it were. My friend Chris Wagg from Church told me that she too had this 'knowing' about my forthcoming illness. I had talked the poor girl into sharing the job of Mediums Booking Secretary at the church. We obviously had to have all yearly planners, dairies etc in duplicate. She went to purchase the two new diaries for next year and then put one back on the shelf - she said she knew she would be doing the job single-handed for a while. In a similar vein I have to mention here a certain bear called Bruno who I acquired in March this year. I've always had a 'penchant' for little furry things (hamsters and teddies and the like) and this one, somewhat larger than usual, looked at me in a certain way from a Garden Centre shelf. I knew I had to have him. I've never felt such an attachment to a bear and 'I just knew' I would need him as a comfort somehow. He was the symbol of both love to come my way and the comfort I was to need. He is always there in very worrying situations and I know that everything will be okay if I just hang on to him. I've never managed to grow up really. I'm not sure now if this is the end of my first childhood or the beginning of my second one! Who cares anyway!

Now, we'll pop back to the events of the 14th October and the summons to Alexandra hospital. It seemed a very long time, the mere 10 minutes I had to wait to see Mr. Purser. It is usual for me in such dire situations for a friend to turn up 'out of the blue.' As I waited my good friend Janet Grainger walked around the corner and sat next to me, she had come for the results of her breast operation the previous week. Timing perfect here or not? - I was the last person she expected to see. Now Janet is a strong medium at times and has helped me through various tough times with her gift. She sat and held my hand only to tell me "Your Mom is here now, you know." Funny, I had a feeling she was somehow!

We went in to see Mr. Purser and, as I knew, the news was rather grim. The news was that there were three tumours on the liver. These were shown up by the scan I had when the other breast lump was shown to be cancerous. We decided to cancel the operation scheduled for the following day. Bruno was there silently fulfilling his

19

usual function and I felt sorry for Mr. Purser and Co. doing the grotty part of their jobs. I remember thinking too, I'm glad it's me and not Steve. Got a feeling I couldn't be so brave if the roles had been reversed! Something made me tell Mr. Purser about the lights and the computer before we set off. I said "Mr. Purser I could write a book". Back came the immediate reply "Shirley write that book, I want the first copy!" He said he would see me the following Wednesday at the Princess Of Wales Hospital adding "And bring the synopsis for that book!" As we walked out I knew I would try to do this. Now is definitely not the time to 'wimp out' of anything - I was now a dog with a bone! The ultimate challenge had been set (They say that we all have at least one book inside us, don't they!)

So you see, if I am being perfectly honest, this situation has not come as a total shock to me. I realise now that Spirit* has been preparing me over the last few years for my present situation. When I look back over my spiritual pathway I can see how it has all pointed me in a certain direction. I feel that, tough as it is, this is still how my pathway should be, this is part of the life of Shirley Anne Bach and now I have to accept it and get on with the job.

We've now reached 16th October and Steve and I have both woken with same sense of purpose. Alternative therapies! Well it's not the human spirit to give up is it? We sat and talked pondering in which areas to look when I 'just knew' that we only had to sit tight for a couple of days and answers would come to us. I never realised how right I was to be!

*Spirit is the part of us that never dies and also the name used for the spirit world. Our Spirit Guide is the person in Spirit who we each have to help us

*\*\*The Third Eye is the 6<sup>th</sup> sense that mediums develop in their training to communicate with Spirit.*

# Childhood and Early Adult Life

I grew up, not five miles from where I now live, in a small drapery shop in Marlbrook, Bromsgrove owned and run by Mom and Dad. The only child and only grandchild on Mom's side. I suppose that I was always the centre of everyone's attention, although they took care not to spoil me in a material way. Brenda, my special friend as I grew up, said to me not long ago "Shirley you weren't just loved, you were cherished" and I do know that indeed I was. Whereas my Mom was also an only child my Dad was one of ten; five boys and five girls, so although lacking in siblings, I did have a grand total of thirty-seven cousins. Nanny Grace, my paternal Grandmother, married when she was eighteen. For the first seven years of married life she fretted over being unable to conceive but at twenty-five her first baby arrived followed by another nine in quite rapid succession – there may well have been more had my grandfather not died in his late thirties of T.B.! Nanny Grace was a good mother and stood no nonsense from any of her children. She was a hard worker and had an assortment of jobs including helping the local midwife and laying out the dead for a doctor in Rubery where she lived. Grace was the only Spiritualist in the entire family and sadly I remember this being regarded with much levity. She regularly attended Bromsgrove Spiritualist Meetings held in a room of The Queens Head public house in Bromsgrove town centre. I reckon that she will be really 'chuffed' that I have chosen to be a Spiritualist too.

The loving and harmonious atmosphere in which I was raised did indeed bring great happiness and joy to me but from a little girl I can remember being profoundly worried by one thing; this business of dying. I just couldn't bear the idea of those I loved so much not being here with me any more and what made it worse was that I felt unable to discuss this with anyone; it being just too awful to contemplate. I would sometimes lie crying in bed over this but I just could not share it. I think that this great need within me was planted there for a reason – my soul just needed to know what comes next, right from when I was small. To me, I have to be honest, if this earthly life is all there is I would sooner not have been born at all; surely all this painstaking effort with its learning and suffering (as well as its joy), must be towards some greater goal otherwise it is a complete waste of time and effort. However, little by little, I have received my evidence of a life after death; I would liken it to collecting the pieces of a puzzle along life's way and in this book I plan to take you along with me showing you as many facets as I can and how they have eventually come together to form a fascinating whole. Why, even at the time of typing the puzzle's pieces are still manifesting and slotting into the overall picture. It is my hope that you will all be able to take something from this book which will lead you to a greater understanding of this earthly life and bring you some of the joy, happiness and sense of purpose which I have felt. Nothing within these pages has been embellished in any way. I have kept a spiritual diary over the last eleven years plus every written message I have been given from 'Bromsgrove Spiritualist Church' so my material was all to hand together with relevant dates and names. I can assure you that this is all true from my perspective. I am not out to impress here; my earnest desire being to share and to help as many as I can.

The first spiritual activity which I recall was when I was about seven. My Mom's Uncle Harold had been in poor health for some time and was in All Saints Hospital at Bromsgrove. A lovely gentle soul he was always particularly fond of my Mom. He called her 'Joey' instead of Joyce and had a habit of putting his fingertips on her shoulders in an affectionate manner. It was a late Winter's afternoon and Mom was playing a small electric organ which we had in the lounge. She was half way through 'Ave Maria' and as she reached the word 'Angels' in the piece she felt fingertips on her right shoulder which pushed her down with such force that I remember the clatter as the music book fell to the floor. Within a quarter of an hour we received a phone call from Harold's daughter to tell us that he had just passed away!

Several years later when Mom, Dad and I moved into my Great Auntie's house after her passing there was another little episode of spiritual activity. As we sat watching T.V. a small brass plate which had belonged to Auntie Annie leaned slightly away from the wall behind the mantelshelf, spun round several times and then fell down flat. As we looked at one another wondering how it could have happened, the matching plate on the other side of the mantelshelf repeated exactly the same manoeuvre.

My first experience of losing someone to the spirit world was not until I reached twenty-one. It was my Granddad and I was absolutely heartbroken. I was unable to listen to any gentle music for months as it just triggered off floods of tears. I remember gleaning not one crumb of comfort from the Church of England funeral service; it was morbid and depressing and left me disconsolate. I've hated 'The Lord's My Shepherd' ever since. This religion just wasn't for me. I needed to know!

From start to finish I just loved school; struggling along with maths and science but doing fine with everything else especially the Arts. Whilst at Secondary school being creative became important to me; anything from drawing, pottery, sculpture and even woodwork (*which I admit to doing in order to avoid p.e.*). Nan and Granddad were both creative by nature. Nan created her own patterns for knitting, sewing and rug making. She had a 'Junk Room' full of stuff for sewing and knitting and this was a real 'Aladdin's Cave' to me. Every weekend we made things together; rag dolls, crocheted blankets; anything from a papier-mache pig to a fine lace doily. Granddad, too, would entertain me by drawing Mickey Mouse or Popeye cartoons quite beautifully and he was '*A Whiz*' at cutting out lettering and designs from folded paper. At school I was to be found regularly in the art rooms during lunch break, finishing off projects or trying something new and I always remember a great compliment paid to me by my Art teacher, Miss Smith. She said; "Shirley I wish I had half of your creative talent"- quite a compliment this and so it came as quite a shock to fail my Art A Level - even the school asked the exam board for a reason but none was forthcoming. I reckon it just wasn't to be – it was not on my pathway to follow art as a career although it has given me great pleasure throughout my life. I am pleased that my son, Paul, has this creative instinct too. From when he was little he always found things to do; never bored but always making and doing. He would spend entire days digging vast holes at the bottom of our garden, making dens and scratting around in the mud to see what could be found and when it became dark he would simply fetch a torch and carry on. When presented with kits of any kind Paul will ignore the instructions and construct something of equal merit of his own. In the year 1999 Steve, Paul and I took one of those train journeys of a lifetime across Queensland, Australia – travelling through the night and seeing the sun rise in a landscape of gum trees and wallabies. But Paul could barely give this his attention; he was far too busy constructing a small model plane from the polystyrene cup that his drink came in! I'm like this too to a certain extent. I have tried to widen my horizons but to be honest I am just as happy at home in my craft room as travelling here, there and everywhere. I have always felt happiness is to be found betwixt the soles of your feet and the top of your head – it's all within and doesn't need searching for elsewhere.

It was during my Secondary School years that I went to a very special person for piano lessons. Joyce Burleigh-Smith, a most unusual and talented lady who taught Art at Redditch College, took piano pupils in her spare time. Grade four piano was as far as I got but Joyce encouraged me no end with various artistic projects too, passing on various skills such as model making and picture framing. She was a real character; her small semi-detached house at one point being home to five dogs, four cats, Zebra Finches and a Mynah bird, not to mention a total of eight pianos, (six upright and two grands). Joyce made beautiful scale models of Romany caravans and of many of the old buildings in Bromsgrove. Avoncroft Museum is now the guardian of these unique treasures and displays them from time to time. So here I had found a very fertile ground for creative enterprises. I sometimes accompanied her to Birmingham Art Gallery where she had her own hanging space and we even took her pictures to London to try for acceptance at the R.S.A open exhibition. Joyce occasionally saw and heard Spirit too. So all in all we were great friends, sharing many interests. Unfortunately Joyce passed away in 1995 with this dratted cancer that plagues so many of us. We really have got to get this dreadful disease sorted!

Leaving school at eighteen my first job was with Birmingham City Council in their personnel department. I stayed here for two years but by then I had had my fill of the place – I'm just not a city person. The last time I went shopping in Birmingham was eighteen years ago when we went to choose wedding rings – I just can't stand the place. I then moved to work at Bromsgrove Magistrates' Court. Here we dealt with a real 'Mish Mash' of humanity as you might imagine and my clerical work would sometimes include going into Court to take licensing fees or occasionally taking notes for my boss, The Clerk to the Justices. The people I worked with here were a great bunch and we did have some laughs. I never wanted to work anywhere else. It was while at the Court, one Friday afternoon when we were up-to-date with our work, that we noticed an advert for consultations with a clairvoyant at the local Perry Hall Hotel *(Now part of Bromsgrove School)*. One by one we sneaked out for a sitting and, looking back, mine was pretty good. The lady told me that I would meet someone in the Autumn, that I would be happily married with one child and live by trees and water. Not bad this – I started seeing Steve (my husband) two months later in October, I have one son, Paul, and my house backs onto Cofton Reservoir! Although I now realise that Mediumship is not about telling fortunes but of proving the after-life, this lady obviously saw a pretty clear picture of my future – that can't be denied. It makes you wonder how much of our life is pre-destined and to what extent free will comes into play. I reckon that life deals us a certain hand but how we play that hand is then our concern. In other words "We cannot Direct the Wind but we can Adjust our Sails".

This creative energy which I have written of, once it has built up, has to be used all the time. It's like having 'a life within a life' as my friend Joyce used to say. I find that if I have been away on holiday and not used this energy for a while, when I return home the ideas and urge to do and make or to play music come tumbling out again and if I don't let them come I am dissatisfied and frustrated. Now, having collected certain skills along life's way, by the time I reached my thirties another urge developed; that this creative energy should be used in some way to help others. It was no longer enough to create, I had to share and allow some benefit to be derived from it all. A turning point came one morning when I scuttled up to my little craft room and from various bits and bobs created a tiny, three-dimensional fairy out of snippings of silver card and white net with delicately dangling legs of cotton and tiny pearl beads for feet. It was the beginning of my card-making phase and I remember Steve saying, "I think you're on to something here Shirl – that's great!" I crafted a few fairy cards which were soon sold and then a friend of a friend asked if she could order some to give to the cast of her drama group when they closed their production of Gilbert & Sullivan's 'Iida'. "Yes," I excitedly responded. "Great", she said, "I'll need forty-two of them". They all had to have 'Iida' and the year in silver on the top and had to be in various shades of pink. It took me days and days. The front room table was a mass of wings and wands, silver snippets and tiny cotton legs. It turned out to be a mammoth task of an exceedingly delicate nature; nobody dared breathe in our front room but it was just what I needed to get my next creative phase on the road.

The same dissatisfaction then began to apply itself to my musical hobby. This is where Bromsgrove Spiritualist Church enters the frame. Once I involved myself here I started to create cards to be sold for Church funds and then I plucked up the courage to play the organ there. I was absolutely terrified before I played for the first time, but my husband has been through this 'nerves thing' as he has played for years in various folk bands and is used to playing in public. "Its just a barrier you have to pass through Shirl – everyone feels the same at first – you can do it!" This is where Steve is a great partner for me, always spurring me on and boosting my confidence which was sadly lacking in my earlier life.

So now life's pattern was beginning to show itself. The pieces of my puzzle were beginning to slot into place. I had arrived at a time and place where my urge to create and share had found a purpose, no matter how humble. I had met, too, a host of great people with whom I could 'Gel' and most importantly I had found out the answer to my life-long question of what happens when we die.

# Mom

There are simply no adequate words here to describe how I loved my Mom. She was my best friend as well as my Mother. We were always 'tuned in' together; each knowing how the other felt without the need for words. Life was going along just fine for all of us before 'the bombshell dropped'. Steve and I were happily settled into our present home at Cofton Hackett and Paul was adored by both sets of grandparents. Connie and Charles, Steve's parents got on so well with my parents and we all came together for Christmas, anniversaries and birthdays. Actually, looking back, it was all a bit too good to be true. There aren't many families who can boast of a perfect blending together – usually someone has to spoil the picture by harbouring grudges or jealousies, but no, life couldn't have been better. In fact I can remember feeling that it was all too good to last – it was as though I had 'a knowing' that our situation was to change; after all if life was this perfect where would the lessons come in. It is the struggles and problems we overcome which form our strengths and character. Mom had developed ovarian cancer; she was diagnosed at sixty-three and passed to spirit at sixty-five.

Those last two years of Mom's life were very intense in every respect. The shock of diagnosis sent us all reeling. Mom had always been glowing with health and energy, forever in the garden, eating healthily and never smoking or drinking. She was the centre of our family life and we all revolved around her. At this time my Nan lived with Mom and Dad and was over ninety. This was all wrong – life's events were upside down and happening in the wrong order. Being told how ill she was was the worst moment of my entire life, much worse than being told of my present demise. It was inconceivable that she shouldn't be here with us enjoying her only grandson who she adored. When I look back I was always so sure that she would live to a ripe old age like my Nan. I would take care of her just as she cared for her Mom. It just shows that we should never take anyone or anything for granted – a life which is sure and steadfast one day can be turned upside down the next. Live each day as though it is your last then there can be no regrets. There is a much mightier force than us in charge of things and we have to bow down to it and various stages of our life no matter how it hurts. My initial reaction was anger with God because I was only able to reason from a limited perspective at this point in my life. I had always felt that there might be a life beyond this but orthodox religion had never been nearly enough for me and it was losing Mom that was the catalyst for requiring spiritual knowledge. I never even had Paul christened as there was a feeling that we should be free to choose our own way of thinking – Paul must find his own way.

I would have moved heaven and earth to save Mom. We went through months of highs and lows. Little steps forward then bigger steps back; operations, recoveries then relapses and more despair, all the while 'clutching at straws'. Mom herself was 'a real brick' throughout her illness. I can honestly say that I never heard a single word of complaint, not in front of me anyway. This may strike you as bizarre but she made a really good job of dying. Come to think of it she made a really good job out of everything she did. I recall her saying to me when I was quite small "Shirley, whatever tasks come your way in life, be they big or small, you can either make a good job of them or a bad one". Well, this wise advice she definitely heeded herself as she bade us farewell in as graceful and dignified a manner as she could muster. What a brave lady – I only hope that I can tear a leaf from her book now that I find myself in a similar situation.

Following her final operation we carried Mom's bed downstairs into the lounge and Dad would sleep beside her on the settee. We buzzed around her like frantic bumblebees doing everything we could think of to cheer her day and bring her pleasure. We tried to tempt her with every tasty morsel imaginable and one day I recall driving all the way to Redditch to 'M&S' for a particular brand of fizzy peach-flavoured water that she had a fancy for. Gradually I filled her room with fresh flowers from her garden; every last vase and pot was employed until Mom finally called me to a halt with; "That's lovely Shirley but please leave my garden alone now".

My Uncle Ron and Auntie Maureen were always there to help us. They often looked after Paul for me and even made a video of all the things they did with him so that we could play it to Mom on T.V. Her heart breaking reaction to this was; "Oh this is grand but *I* should be doing these things with Paul". This was the nearest to complaining that she ever came, within my earshot anyway.

I must mention here a particular moment when I was caring for Mom. I closed my eyes and in my own head I said, "God, I love her so much, why does she have to go somewhere else?" I suppose it was what we could term a silent and fervent prayer and one that incredibly I was to receive back *word for word* at Bromsgrove Spiritualist Church less than four months later. I still possess the message which was written down for me at the time, as most messages are at Church. Ponder this awhile reader. A prayer, i.e. a sincere plea from the heart, was registered by the spirit world and relayed back to me through a medium *'word perfect.'* It had never even been spoken out loud but was felt, thought, sent and received then relayed back to me in its exact original form. Wow!

In the midst of crisis situations humour often raises its head. This is illustrated by the last words I heard spoken by Mom. She had long since declined food and was now even struggling to drink from a glass, so one of our visiting nurses suggested we use a straw. As we administered the first drink in this new manner Dad announced "IT'S A STRAW JOYCE, A STRAW". One eye flickered open briefly "Yes I know it is," she whispered, "I'm not bloody daft you know". Indeed it is all too easy to believe that because someone is winding down from this life and tuning in to the next, which is after all what the process of dying is, that they have lost their mental capacities. Not so, every feeling and thought and all that they have ever learned, is still stored within; they are as complete at this time as they will ever be. Everything within is ready within the storehouse of the soul, to be transported with their 'Etheric Body' to the next stage of existence. I always think of death as the only trip you go on where you don't have to pack – it's all there at the ready. This etheric counterpart to our physical body is attached by a cord of light to the physical somewhere down by our feet (so we are informed by Spirit). Death is the moment when the cord is severed and we are released leaving our body or old overcoat behind us. There is a parallel here with birth if you stop to consider it. There you were all snug and warm in the womb, quite oblivious of the wider world until you are pushed out and the umbilical cord is cut. Death too is a form of birth into a wider existence which we can only have a limited grasp of at present because we are limited by our current physical senses. Always remember, too, that hearing is the very last sense to go so never whisper anything that you don't want the dying person to hear.

I wasn't with Mom when she finally took her transition to Spirit and this is often the case. They cling to earthly life – your love for them and their's for you, acting like a magnet. It is often much easier for them to set off on their journey when you are not around. So never feel guilty about being absent for a passing, they probably couldn't manage it while you were with them. In any case when we take our transition we are always met by loved ones from the other side and escorted. We are never alone.

Despite the acute suffering that we all experienced during Mom's illness, Mom in a physical sense and the rest of us because we loved her so much, it was a time when we gave of our very best to one another. At the end of the day suffering brings with it an infinite capacity for the loving, caring hearts of people to be expressed. The kindness of folk in times like these is wonderful and overwhelming. It sustains and uplifts you. It is a time of pulling out all the stops, getting into top gear – you can't afford to waste time now on petty, unimportant matters.  Like me now, you suddenly realise that **YOU ONLY HAVE TIME FOR THE IMPERATIVES!**

# Apres Mom

I just did not want to face Mom's funeral on 5<sup>th</sup> May, 1993. I have never had such an urge to run away from anything in my entire life but I knew I had to be there with Dad. We held hands all the way through and he was so composed and dignified that I managed it too, somehow. Strength is always forthcoming from somewhere when you need it. Removing my glasses helped too; the whole affair passing by in a hazy blur. The one vital thing I gleaned at that funeral was the certainty that wherever Mom was she was definitely not in that coffin. I 'just knew'. This was the starting point of my search. Where had Mom gone? None of this "have faith and trust in the Almighty that one day I would see her again." I was going to get down to the nitty gritty of the afterlife divested from all the creeds and dogmas which we are spoon-fed with throughout childhood and that had never helped me in the past. If there is an afterlife then everything must have a concrete scientific explanation and this is what I needed.

In retrospect, I feel that Mom was well prepared by Spirit for her passing. About ten months prior to passing she told me that she had seen a little girl through her bedroom window in the middle of the night. She had woken to a full moon gleaming through and felt drawn to open the curtains and look out. The little girl, who she said looked as solid as she did, wore her hair in two long plaits and a 1940's style gabardine mac. She walked along the pavement trailing an old-fashioned tricycle behind her before just 'disappearing' into the hedge. Mom said that she instinctively knew that the child was not of this earth had she believed her to be real she would undoubtedly have gone outside to see why she was wandering about in the early hours. Checking the date, we realised that this had occurred on Midsummer's Night. I feel also that my Mother did possess a spiritual maturity and had probably learned all her lessons here on the earth plane. Wisdom, serenity and courage are words that spring to mind here.

Now we arrive at a strategic turning point in my life; my first trip to Bromsgrove Spiritualist Church. There was absolutely no dithering – I saw an advert for the place in the local newspaper and I HAD TO GO. I telephoned Steve at work to check that he would be at home that night to look after Paul. His initial response was, "You'll be on your own – you won't know anybody". This did not matter one jot. I said I just knew I had to be there. Walking in through those church doors, the place busy and buzzing with friendly chatter, I immediately felt at home in the warmth of the place. A lady called Joan, who I have now known for nearly twelve years, told me that as soon as she cast eyes on me that night she felt that I belonged and would be staying. We opened in prayer then sang The Lord's Prayer and then the Medium spoke on spiritual philosophy in which I got quite engrossed. We sang a rousing hymn and then the Medium, Margaret Barrett, took the platform again and began her demonstration of mediumship.

This lady's first words astounded me – nearly knocked me off my chair. She said: "I've got Joyce here". With no self-consciousness at all I shouted up "That's my Mom. She continued: "Well, if this lady is for you she is telling me that you know someone who has just lost their dog". Yes, I did – my friends and neighbours Diane and Kevin had lost their old dog the same week that Mom had gone. She continued to say that it was "a mixed border collie, much loved and very grey around the muzzle" adding that the dog was now with Len in the spirit world; a gent who wore a flat cap. This was all 'spot on'. I was just amazed. The only part of the message I didn't recognise was the name 'Len' but when I mentioned all this to Diane, somewhat tentatively as you might imagine, she said that Len was Kevin's Granddad and that he did indeed wear a flat cap. **THIS WAS IT. I HAVE BEEN HOOKED ON SPIRIT EVER SINCE!** The lady I sat next to at Church that first night was a medium herself called Elsie Hollis. She said that Mom was obviously very eager to make contact, as she was first in the queue and it was my first visit. She promised that if I continued to attend Church I would be sure to receive a lot more. How right she was.

I went regularly to Church after this and not just to await the next contact from Mom. I liked the people and found the philosophy portion of the service, we call it the address, really interesting. After about six weeks of attendance a Medium called Pauline Essex served the Church. She had come from Tamworth to be with us. She came directly to me with a message from Mom and I feel it would be worthwhile here to take you through this communication which I still have written down amongst my 'shoe box full' of collected spirit messages. Indeed this particular one is the most treasured little slip of paper that I possess. The opening part of the communication, exactly as I had written down for me in note form, reads: -

*Sadness – bottling up – let it go. Grieving needs to be done. Lady arms around you, pulling you to her – "Come on, come on you'll get through. A lot relied on her – taken from the middle like a leaning post.*

This was all true. I had a lot of tears to let go of – we did, as a family, rely on her. She was indeed the centre of our lives – we revolved around her.

The next section read: -

*She is alright now – free from pain. Someone didn't get there on time – she knew there was a reason. She didn't want them to be any more upset. Bed coming and going – praying for her – they were hanging onto her. She couldn't take any more.*

The one who didn't get there at the end was Mom's best and life-long friend Audrey who would definitely have been there for her if her own Mother had not been taking her transition to spirit at the same time. The coming and going in bed refers to her drifting in and out of consciousness and we were indeed holding on to her with love and prayers.

*Remember me – the photos – chair. "I do hope she's alright and being taken care of"*

This section was the most evidential to me. Several days prior to this message I had gone down into my lounge in the middle of the night and was looking through a batch of photos, mainly of Mom and Dad with grandson Paul. There was a particular print with Mom sat in an armchair nursing Paul in her arms and as I looked at it I just sobbed and sobbed and I said out loud to her "I hope you are alright and being taken care of". As in my previous chapter, here was my sincere and heartfelt prayer being relayed back to me, not only in sentiment but verbatim! It was just so hard loving and caring for someone for so long and then not knowing where or how they were. I really needed this. The photo of Mom in the chair which had triggered my outburst of grief, was thoughtfully framed by Steve the very next day and has remained on my mantelpiece ever since.

The next section of the message referred to a neighbour and I was not sure about this bit. However, the last section read: -

*Kent – "Maybe its because I'm a Londoner" – Scotland. November Celebration for child – piano from the lady.*

The Medium said that she was given "Kent" and then heard Mom singing "Maybe its because I'm a Londoner". This was correct because Steve was down in London at the time of this message and the actual building he was staying in was in Kent Street. I had been discussing a trip to Scotland that same day with a friend over the telephone and my son's birthday is the 8th November. Often Spirit leave a "Gift" for you before they go; often a specific flower but mine from Mom was a piano – I've always had a piano and play most days.

I was up on 'cloud nine' after this Church service. It had literally made the hairs stand up on the back of my neck. I parked my car safely on the drive back home but I didn't remember the journey. My mind was in a whirl. **IT WAS TRUE. WE DO LIVE ON SOMEWHERE ELSE – WE DON'T DIE.** Now life would never be the same. I rang around all of my friends and relations to pass this momentous news on. My Dad was quite overwhelmed when I presented him with my treasured little slip of paper and from then on he was really keen to know how Church services had gone.

Life for me was different after this. O.K I had to accept that I could no longer have Mom on a physical level but I now knew that she was somewhere else, complete and whole and that GOD HAD NOT WASTED HER. What was more, one day we would be re-united. So far from pining away I just got on with my life and soon found that the old adage 'When one door closes another one opens' to be true. I've certainly learned to stand on my own two feet more, whereas I was very reliant on Mom. I know that I would not have grown so much spiritually, if I had not lost her to spirit. Her best friend, Audrey, and I filled a space for one another too, going on shopping sprees and outings and supporting each other as we have done for the past eleven years.

Again there is a paradox here. If I hadn't lost a fantastic Mom who meant the world to me I would never have met the great friends I've made at Bromsgrove Spiritualist Church. We can't have everything in life can we? Leastways not all at the same time. Life is a pattern of loved ones here, losing people to spirit and then loving the ones over there, just as they continue to love you until they come to fetch you and you are all together again. Thus existence, from the wider spiritual perspective, is a series of loving, letting go, moving on and then waiting for others to catch you up. All the while hopefully, learning, maturing and widening our soul experience.

Those first few weeks after losing Mom I was so angry with God. Now, I can see that whatever happens to us is all in the plan and that the really bad experiences we have are really opportunities to grow and learn and often we need to have them to lead us on to pastures new.

# Spiritualist Church

I want to try here to show you why attending a Spiritualist Church is so rewarding and positive. What is it that makes it so different to other religions? Well for a start, it's not just a religion but also a combination of religion, philosophy and science. We find people from various faiths coming through our doors and often staying. Sometimes, like myself, they come as a result of bereavement because their faith cannot satisfy their questions and they are searching. Others come because they see spirit; perhaps it frightens them or they don't know how to control it or 'Turn if off' as it were. We have an on-going awareness class at 'Bromsgrove Spiritualist Church' where people can learn how to control and use spiritual gifts, often bringing them to fruition so that they can be used to benefit others. Spiritual gifts are given for a reason and should be used for the betterment of others. Jesus had them in great strength and abundance and achieved wonderful results with them but he should not be looked upon as the only one. People throughout the ages and today are given spiritual gifts to use for the benefit of humanity. It has been the orthodox churches that have suppressed and condemned contact with the spirit world through their desire to hold onto power and keep the people 'under their thumb'. It has all been about controlling people and denying them the realisation of the great power that lies latent within all of us.

When you enter a Spiritualist Church you are not being dictated to. You listen and glean evidence and it is up to you what you take from it. Everyone must make their individual journey and it will not be the same route for all. There is also the big plus of not listening to the same person every service. We are served by around 120 different mediums each year at our Church. Each one brings their own perspective on the Spirit World and giving their philosophy with a variety of styles and approaches. Services are as varied and interesting as the different people who stand on our platform. Every month or so we have evenings of Mediumship where the entire night is given over to Spirit communications. These are usually advertised locally and bring in a wide spectrum of the general public. For some of them it will be a one-off experience but others will be given that little nugget of evidence which lures them back wanting to know more. They often return to attend services and begin learning from the philosophy.

To comfort the bereaved by proving life-after-death is our main aim. I just don't know where I would be in my life now if I hadn't been led to Spiritualism. Proof of survival provides a link, no matter how tenuous it seems, with those you have loved and lost. Initially the messages from spirit can be the main reason for your attendance at Church and this is quite understandable because it is tangible proof that someone you have loved is not lost but simply 'elsewhere' in another dimension. However, if you pass beyond this stage you will find the philosophy and science of the subject utterly absorbing. As I said before, once you're hooked, that's it – there lies ahead of you a lifetime of learning both in this world and the next. I have found that I can often go for months without receiving any communications from Spirit but this generally means that life if ticking along alright. It is when you have a real need or reach an important turning point in earthly life that Spirit will not let you down. During this present crisis in my life they are literally propelling me through and guiding me every day.

You will notice that there is, and indeed should be, much mirth in a Spiritualist Church because it mirrors life itself. If you arrive expecting to sit in the dark in a very serious atmosphere to 'call up the dead' you will be very surprised. Those from the Spirit realms come of their own volition on a vibration of love. The Medium is there as a telephone link between the two worlds, nothing more. Neither is Spiritualism a 'Quick Fix'. You may be given just enough proof, like I was, to grab your attention on your first visit; just enough to arouse your curiosity and make you ask, "Where is all this information coming from?" It takes tenacity and perseverance to learn of the Spirit realms. In fact, it is akin to life itself 'the more you are prepared to put in the more you will get out'.

Once you have learned enough to make it apparent to you that life is continuous you will understand that you still have a relationship with those on the other side of life. They are aware of what you are doing in your life and will come through with advice and support. They help you to take life's knocks and not to give up. When I pass to Spirit I want my parents to say, "Well done Shirl, you did your best".

Now why not change the perspective here and consider all of this from the point of view of those in the Spirit world. You've just passed over and you are desperate to let your folks know that you have arrived, you feel well again and THAT THERE IS NO SUCH THING AS DEATH. You can see and hear your loved ones here but they just don't register that you are there unless they are mediumistic of course. Imagine the sheer frustration! The only way they will be able to communicate with you is if you are in the presence of a Medium. Every so often we get a really tenuous Spirit link to someone in our congregation. You may be the recipient because you live five doors down from someone's second cousin, but spirit can be so desperate to link that they will zoom in on you hoping that you will pass a message on to their loved one. I am remembering here the rather morose spirit in the film 'Ghost' who haunted the underground and how Sam Malone begged him to teach him the art of moving an aluminium can so that he would be able to attract the attention of those on earth. *(A great film 'Ghost' and rather well researched I felt)*. So don't we owe it to our loved ones to put ourselves occasionally in a position where they can contact us, either by going to a Spiritualist Church or by a private consultation with a medium? Remember it works both ways, this communication business.

Another very important aspect of what we do at Spiritualist Church is the healing. Susan Sprigg, our healing leader, has a team of qualified healers who carry out their work after our Wednesday service. They are also prepared to make home visits where necessary or go out to hospitals. Healers are mediums too; they form a link between earth and spirit but instead of receiving and passing on messages they are concerned with the passing on of healing energy. Susan often sums up the process as 'From Spirit – through Spirit – to Spirit'. Healers penetrate your aura, (the energy field that we all have around our body), and often use hands on healing as well. To appreciate how spiritual healing takes effect we have to understand that within our physical body we have an 'etheric' or spirit body. This is the part of us that moves on to the next dimension when we shed the physical one and 'die'. It is also the 'blueprint' for our physical form and if we can correct this blueprint the physical body can often cast off illness or disease. It takes years to qualify as a healer under 'The Spiritualists National Union'. A strict code of conduct is adhered to and all S.N.U. healers are fully insured. Healing goes alongside conventional medicine and is concerned with making the whole person feel better. Spiritual healing can cure but often it is about creating a peace within so that patients are more able to cope with their problem. Healing can also be of great help to those who are about to pass to spirit taking away the fear and making transition more peaceful. If it is someone's time to pass then healing cannot alter this course – as it states in the Lords Prayer, which is included in all our services, "Thy Will be Done".

I want to share with you now an experience of healing which I received two years ago whilst suffering with chickenpox. 'Suffering' being the operative word here – I was in an awful state; spots on eyelids, throat, down gullet, everywhere! I felt so awful that I couldn't even bear the sight of myself so it became my habit to wait for nightfall and take my bath by candlelight. On the night in question after lowering myself gingerly into the water I can honestly say that I never felt so miserable in my entire life. I was sore and itching and felt 'at rock bottom'. As I lay there a strange sensation worked its way up from my toes, spreading upwards in what I can only describe as a warm wave of energy. It was a surge of power and inner warmth and I found my outlook had changed and my spirit lift as it pervaded me. It was not until the following day when Mel Clark, our Church President, phoned to see how I was and said: "We sent you some special healing last night, did you feel it?" Boy had I felt it! I hadn't even thought about it being a Wednesday and yes it was about 7.45 when I took my bath; the time the healing is always sent.

Spiritualism encompasses all of humanity in its beliefs. At the end of the day it matters not whether you are a Buddhist, a Sikh, a Christian or a Jehovah's Witness; everyone is part of 'The Brotherhood of Man,' which is our second principle. Nobody is better than anyone else but maybe just at a different stage in his or her spiritual development and on a different pathway. You can take what you feel is useful to you from other religious beliefs as long as it helps you to live a better life. If anything, Spiritualism has made some of the happenings in the Bible more plausible to me and although I don't consider Jesus as the Son of God, for we are all sons and daughters of God, I do see him as the greatest healer and Medium who ever lived. Also, realising some of the wonderful communications and manifestations of Spirit, you can grasp more clearly how some of the miracles in the Bible took place. I do not believe either that Jesus died for our sins. Our sins are our own concern and must be paid for in the next sphere of existence before we can progress spiritually. Jesus did set us a wonderful example, however, and the world would be a better place if we had followed in his footsteps. Our 6$^{th}$ principle at Church is 'Compensation and Retribution for all good and evil deeds done on earth' – in other words one day we will all get our just desserts for the manner in which we have lived our earthly life. If everyone heeded this then Mans' behaviour would improve in leaps and bounds and this planet would be a far better place.

If your religion makes you a better person and leads you successfully along your spiritual pathway then it is the right way for you. The majority of the world's problems stem from an intolerance of each other's different beliefs. I would never dream of suggesting to a devout Christian or Muslim that Spiritualism is superior to their religion, it is just where I have found my home. I will never forget the reaction I had once when I told a stranger that I was a Spiritualist. It was at a particularly painful stage in my life. Steve and I had just lost both of our fathers within three days of each other, and Steve's Mom, Connie, was in hospital about to undergo a life threatening operation. We couldn't even tell Connie that her own husband had passed because of upsetting her prior to her 'op'. I entered the hospital chapel to be quiet with my own thoughts when a middle-aged woman joined me. She said, "isn't it a beautiful place?" and I agreed with her, it was. She then went on to say that Christianity brings so much comfort to you in life. I said, "Well, yes it does to many but I am a Spiritualist". She moved away from me like I had some contagious disease informing me that contact with the 'Dead' was wicked and then said to Steve that she hoped I hadn't contaminated him with my wicked ways. I was really upset; I had entered that Chapel to try and take stock and calm myself. HOW DARE SHE PASS JUDGEMENT ON ME LIKE THAT! I would imagine that, like a lot of people who so arrogantly pass judgement on the subject, that she has never so much as set foot in a Spiritualist Church. I gave her her 'come-uppance' and marched out of the Chapel. So I say 'each to his own' – as long as you don't feel it is right to kill, maim or hurt others in the name of your religious beliefs and you realise that love is the key to everything then you are doing just fine. You don't need to have any belief system at all. As long as you're a good person you will still end up in the same afterlife with those who have diligently attended Church services because we are all part of the same Natural Law.

We welcome a complete cross-section of people at our Spiritualist Church, from gentle elderly ladies to young lads bearing tattoos and earrings and that is just the way we like it. I would hate to be without the real 'gems' of friends that I've made there and we have such fun while we're running the Church. Sometimes we organise such events as skittles evenings and I mustn't forget to mention here our two panto productions, the last being 'The Wizard of Oz' featuring the most gorgeous 15 stone Dorothy you could ever wish to see. There is a great sense of belonging and pulling together for something really worthwhile. I don't think as human beings we can be truly happy and fulfilled unless we are giving to others. We need to serve others. If you stop to think, it is the times in our life when we are too self-centred and wrapped up in ourselves when we are at our unhappiest. Love has to flow all the time – it's just the natural way of life. It's what we're here for.

# Proof Undeniable

In this chapter I would like to illustrate the different types of spiritual communication which has given me such proof over the last 11 years. Most have come via Mediums by way of messages at Church, but some have reached me by way of personal experiences and yet more information has been gleaned from relatives, friends and neighbours. I have found that once you start to talk openly on this subject many people have had their own spiritual experiences and are only too eager to share them with you.

The most dramatic spiritual contacts I have had the privilege to go through came in the form of two out-of-the-body experiences. The first was on the 2nd February, 1997. I had just got settled in bed and finished turning from side to side, as you do, to get comfortable when I was lifted up in a vortex. It was very powerful, pulling me upwards. I was literally breathless with amazement. As I gained height in this spiralling motion I saw very clearly with the third eye a bright silver slim crescent moon in a dark sky before 'going into reverse' and unwinding in this vortex then falling back down and into my body. I actually remember putting out my hands to steady myself as I 'came in to land'. I sat up in bed, Steve being still sound asleep, and mentally asked: - "Did that really happen?" As if by way of confirmation I was shown a series of beautiful lights which rotated around on the bedroom ceiling- silvers, pinks and golds. I always know when I am seeing with the third eye as I am so short-sighted that without my specs normal vision is really blurred and fuzzy, so anything glimpsed with the third eye is crystal clear despite my not wearing any. Speaking from my own experience, there is absolutely nothing whispy or misty about anything seen clairvoyantly – it is usually well-defined and sharp; in fact this is where the word 'clairvoyant' comes from – literally meaning 'clear-seeing'. After returning to my body in bed I felt breathless and almost winded by my 're-entry'. As soon as Steve woke up I obviously told him of my 'little journey'. It being February and the alarm going off really early, it was still very dark. Steve, every practical in his approach, drew back the bedroom curtains to reveal the sky. There was the moon in its thin crescent phase just as I had been shown it. I had been totally unaware of the moon's phase. The medium I was sitting in circle with at this time was Ann Taylor and I phoned her that morning to impart the story of my strange trip to her. She explained that my spirit body has taken me up through the ceiling and roof of my house so that the night sky was visible to me. Because my spirit body would have been vibrating so fast it would not recognise the physical barriers of the roof etc. which is vibrating at its dense low earthly rate and I had thus been able to pass right through it.

On the 1st July, 1997 I was in for a similar experience. This second trip, however, started when I was in sleep state because I woke up and was 'out of my body' again, this time standing at the top of our staircase. My Mom was standing at the foot of the stairs looking really well and dressed in everyday clothes, *(I even recognised the pink and grey shirt she was wearing – it was the same one she wore in that photo of her nursing Paul in the chair)*. She stood smiling at me arms open and outstretched and beckoned me: - "Come on Shirley, come on" It was at this point that I felt the strong pulling and travelling in a vortex back into my body just like before. I distinctly remember trying to shout "Steve" but no sound would come from my mouth. Again, I was left almost winded and short of breath. Like before, I mentally asked Spirit "Did that really happen?" Then, as before, came the beautiful shapes and colours twirling around on the bedroom ceiling, again seen clearly with the third eye – this being obvious again as no glasses were worn. I phoned Anne again and she confirmed that this was another O.B.E. but that this time I was taken to the Spirit Dimension to see my Mom. I will mention here that three weeks prior to this second experience I was told by medium Hugh Davies at our Wednesday service that I was to do some more astral travelling as this was part of my spiritual development. He also told me never to be afraid as I would always be guided safely back into my body.

These out-of-the body experiences would seem to be far from rare. My elderly neighbour and good friend Nan Buggins remembers quite distinctly leaving her body when she was ill and passed out in her hallway. She lives on her own and after fainting completely lost track of time, but the experience she had whilst 'out of it' remains vivid to her to this day. She told me that she was taken down a beautiful tunnel of colours to reach a light at the other end. There she saw an unspeakably beautiful land with the people she had loved and lost waiting for her. She said she really yearned to stay there but was told that it was not her time yet and sent whirling back down the tunnel into her earthly overcoat. This trip had a profound effect on her and has never faded from her mind. In fact it is strange that these experiences stay so clearly in the mind and don't fade like dreams or ordinary earthly experiences. I think it must be that they are important to your soul journey and have to stay with you. Nan recalls discussing her experience with her next-door neighbour, Gideon, who at this time, was Hospital Chaplain of Rubery Hill Hospital, near Birmingham. He showed great interest and then told her of his own similar out-of-the-body experience. Twice Gideon had been seriously injured in first a motorbike accident and secondly in a car collision. On both occasions he told Nan how he had been taken down a beautiful tunnel to be greeted at the other end by those who had passed before him. Gideon described what he saw as a beautiful garden and wanted to stay, but on both occasions he too was told that it was not his time yet and sent back. Apparently he was not a cleric at the time of these two experiences but these glimpses of the after life were to prove the motivation for him to 'Take to the cloth.' He was vicar of Holy Trinity Church, Lickey for several years. Likewise my Aunty Audrey (one of Dad's sisters), who we very nearly lost with bowel cancer about 40 years ago, tells of the same tunnel experience and being sent back.

Sceptics are apt to dismiss O.B.Es as hallucination caused by chemical reactions in the dying brain but I have always asked myself why all seem to have the same hallucination. This little mystery, however, has just been cleared up for me. I am currently reading a book about Stephen Turoff, the world-famous psychic surgeon. His guide gives an explanation for the 'tunnel experience' during a trance lecture. Our etheric or spirit body is attached to the physical by a cord of light which is to be found down by the feet. When we take our transition to spirit the etheric body slips from the physical and travels down this cord ready to be released to the spirit world. The last part of us to slip from our body is the consciousness or etheric brain and it, too, travels down the cord of light which we see as a tunnel as we travel down it. The point of no return is when the cord is severed from the physical, so it is possible to nearly pass to spirit and experience this journey but if the cord remains attached to the physical then its not your time to go. Brilliant this, isn't it – a real little gem!

The most tangible evidence I have received from Spirit took place one afternoon towards the end of November, 1995. I was alone in my kitchen preparing the evening meal. The heavy glass lid of the glass casserole I was using was lying flat on the kitchen worktop. Without being touched, it started to shift in a controlled manner, moving about three inches upwards, back to the centre, three inches downwards and then the same distance to right and then left. It had moved so precisely describing the four points of the compass as it did so. I had this feeling that it might be Mom and I asked out loud if she was playing tricks on me. As though in instant reply the glass lid repeated the whole procedure over again in exactly the same manner. Two days later as I worked in the same place the lid flew up off a bottle of still lemon juice with such gusto that it hit the ceiling. On 17th December, which was Mom's birthday, I attended Church only to receive a message from Mom together with a good description of her. The message was that 'Her Spirit has made its presence felt in my home recently'.

Spirit help can be of a really practical nature and this has been forthcoming during several really difficult phases of my life. About six months after losing Mom I was finding life rather a strain. Paul was a lively five year old and at least three days a week I went to Dad's house to help him. After all Nan was 92 now and becoming increasingly frail. The domestic situation was not an easy one as Nan was now prey to dizzy spells and needing help of a personal nature – remember Dad was her son-in-law not her son so there were certain tasks that only I could do for her. I was striving to replace Mom in Nan's eyes (she even used to call me Joyce by mistake), trying to help Dad as much as I could with house and garden and then running my own home too. I had reached a certain pitch and felt that all this effort was unsustainable. I attended the Sunday service at Bromsgrove Spiritualist Church and medium Ted Freeth came to me and said that Spirit knew that I was finding life a strain and that "in February a burden would be taken from me". Now although I didn't think of Nan as being a burden and indeed loved her very much, I did wonder if this message meant that I was to lose her. When we reached the 27th February for some reason I was reminded of Ted Freeth's message and I realised that Nan had not altered her will since my Mother's passing. Nan agreed that the will ought to be re-written and on that same day I re-wrote it and we asked two neighbours in to witness it. *(It's often so simple to write a will that I really can't see why people waste their money on Solicitors here)*. Both Dad and Nan felt happy that this task was done. The next day, the last day of February, I was to receive an urgent phone call from Dad. Nan had fallen in her room and couldn't move. Sadly her hip was broken and she was hospitalised. As her next of kin I had to sign the consent for an immediate operation to insert a pin. Within a week my Nan had passed with pneumonia. How helpful Ted Freeth's message had been here. Nan's will was sorted just in the nick of time. Mind you when I did the Probate on Nan's small estate I was rather worried that the authorities would accuse me of pushing her over on the day after she had re-made her will, making me one of the main benefactors. How could I possibly have explained that I had received guidance from 'the World Beyond'?

Those of you who have children will probably be aware that from time to time as they grow up they occasionally 'go off the rails'. My son Paul had just 'blotted his copybook' in a manner that had really upset me and I was at the end of my tether with him. It was a Sunday and I had been very upset both by what he had done and the ensuing family row. That day it was my turn to chair our Service at Church and I told Paul that I didn't feel I could stand on the platform, I was just too distraught. He surprised me by offering to come with me and help so off we went, *(me with eyes still red and face blotchy)*. When we arrived at Church it was not the advertised medium whom I had expected, as she was ill. Medium Richard Foster had stepped into her shoes for the evening. Paul and I busied ourselves setting out glasses and jugs of water, lighting candles and putting up the hymn numbers. I fully expected Paul to amuse himself in the back hall during the service (as he had done before), but no, he went into church and sat himself down on the front row. Richard's address during the first part of the service included quite a lot about children and young people and their place in society and parts of it were certainly pertinent to Paul. We then started the mediumship and with his first contact Richard went straight to Paul saying "I'd like to speak to the young man on the front row please". The two spirit people who he could see with Paul were, without any shadow of a doubt, his grandparents (Steve's Mom and Dad). His description of them was plain even to Paul, especially when he said that the lady was exceptionally tall and had a bad foot which she dragged behind her – stressing that it was a problem with the one foot only, not both. Now Connie who was 6ft tall damaged her ankle badly years before I knew her and due to insufficient physiotherapy the muscles in her one ankle wasted away hence she always had to drag her one foot along after her. Having established the identity of his spirit visitors Richard went on to tell Paul that his grandparents were describing him as 'a bicycle' and continued, "This here bicycle is a really super machine but at the moment its handle bars are twisted and its saddle is facing the wrong way. It needs sorting out and you had better do it because at present it is not going in the right direction".

Let's just stop for a moment to consider how helpful and appropriate this spirit communication was and how the spirit world put themselves out to arrange everything for the evening. Firstly the booked medium had been forced to cancel at the last minute and the medium who replaced her has always been particularly interested in children and young people. You often find as you listen to mediums that they have their own special interests and Richard Foster's is definitely the welfare of the young. Secondly, consider how unusual it was for Paul to offer to accompany me to Church – indeed you could have knocked me down with a feather when he did. Then for him to sit right under Richard's nose on the front row. Paul never said much after this and I thought it best to leave well alone but I believe that it made him stop and think.

With spirit contact it is often the strange and seemingly trivial proof which is the most convincing. Those little odds and ends of life which would mean nothing to anyone else but could not have been guessed at or included in any generalisations. I will take the time here to illustrate a few such little gems. The first was the little blue bed jacket given to me by medium Glenys Owen soon after Mom passed. That little jacket was her favourite and had to be washed and tumble dried each day so that she could always wear it. Then there was 'The Lonely Little Petunia in an Onion Patch' given to me by the wonderful medium Val Smith from Stourbridge. This was a silly little song my Dad regaled me with when I was small. It was also Val who gave me the sweets called 'Fisherman's Friends' during a message from Steve's Dad just days after his passing and prior to his funeral. You know that awful hospital plastic bag that you are given when somebody has died in hospital which contains their personal belongings, well Steve and I were unlucky enough to have two of them in our garage waiting to be sorted, one from Steve's Dad who passed on 23$^{rd}$ January, 1998 and one from my Dad who followed him three days afterwards on the 26$^{th}$. I never knew how 'spot on' Val's communication was at the time she gave it, but a couple of days later when we tackled those bags what was the only item in Steve's Dad's coat pocket? Yes, you've guessed it, an unopened packet of 'Fisherman's Friends'! My Mother-in-law Connie once impressed medium Nick Burford to describe, in the air, the shape of her favourite vase. It was concave; wide at top and bottom and narrow in the middle. Now I had numerous cut glass vases which had once belonged to her and on returning home I asked Steve if she had had a favourite and he pointed straight to the concave one. I have kept flowers in this one ever since. In similar vein a medium called Bryan Allport once gave me a very precise nugget of evidence when he brought through to me a traffic warden with a mole on the side of his face. This chap used to be a regular visitor to the Court when he handed in the Fixed Penalty tickets.

Now we will move on to a rather different aspect of spirit communication - Spirit Art. I have seen several mediums who work in this way but at Bromsgrove Spiritualist Church we are very lucky to have our own artist by the name of Gerald Townsend-Howes. Gerald has had no art training whatsoever and he always tells everyone at the start of his demos that he couldn't draw a portrait of anyone to save his life. He can only do this under the influence of the Spirit world. He does not see the spirit visitors he draws but is just impressed to place certain marks upon the paper. In other words his hands just know what to do. But Gerald is only half of a team, the other half (also his 'better half') is his wife Sue. Sue and Gerald's' romance blossomed at Bromsgrove Spiritualist Church and spirit obviously had a hand in this as Sue is an experienced medium and the pair of them work extremely well together. Gerald's spiritual gifts have only really unfolded since he has been with Sue. When he first set foot in Church on his own none of this was apparent; in fact he was rather shy and liked to blend into the background but Spirit obviously had other ideas for him. So far I have been the fortunate recipient of four of Gerald's drawings, all of which I recognised with ease together with matching evidence. The one which was extremely evidential, and not just to me, was one of my Uncle John who passed with leukaemia. I began to recognise him when Gerald had drawn just the eyes. I knew without a shadow of a doubt when Sue tuned in and said that he sent all his love to Jean on the earth plane. Jean is my Dad's sister, who was married to John. Most of the evidence which accompanied the drawing I was able to accept there and then but there were three things that I was unable to take. Now, as I've said before, the evidence which you receive and have to go away and investigate is very sound, after all no mind reading is possible if the information is not in your mind in the first place. When I later showed Aunty Jean the drawing and accompanying information the three items which puzzled me she could accept straight away. Firstly Sue had told me that John came through to her with Alsatian dogs. Now I knew he and Jean had once had a boxer dog but what I wasn't aware of was that when they first met John had been a dog handler in the R.A.F. and worked with Alsatians. The second matter was that Sue saw an oxygen cylinder with him at his passing; I didn't know that oxygen was administered before he 'popped off' but it was. Thirdly I was given the sound of a recorder being played through a hedge. On hearing this Aunty Jean smiled – "Oh" she said, "The little girl whose garden backed onto ours was fond of John and she made him listen to every new recorder tune she had learned through the hedge". This was certainly Spirit communication at its best!

Spirit contact can often bring with it overwhelming emotion and I will write here of the most moving of my many experiences. It took place the year after losing my Dad. I had been on a residential weeklong course at  Stansted Hall in Essex *(this being the headquarters of the Spiritualists National Union)*. I was really relaxed having enjoyed a week of spiritual lessons and meditations with no T.V., newspapers etc. It was the day after returning home and I was upstairs putting away laundry, still basking in the lovely tranquillity I had brought back with me from Stansted. As I turned my head there was my Dad smiling at me. He was at the side of me in my peripheral vision; somewhere between my head and the room I was in *(it's so hard to explain)*. He was so solid and he beamed at me looking really well and happy. He stayed just long enough to deliver his smile and then was gone, but the most overwhelming aspect of this was the feeling of love he brought with him. I felt bowled over by it as though my heart was going to burst. As usual, I reached for the phone and Ann Taylor: "Well, Shirley", she said, "now you realise how wonderful it is to be touched by spirit".

So you see Spirit has sent evidence in many different ways. During this present time of my illness they are extremely busy with me and I can feel their energy around me most of the time – this must be why I'm managing to stay so cheerful much of the time. One of the first spiritual happenings during my present illness occurred on the night when my surgeon, Mr. Purser, had told me that my cancer had come back on site. At the time I was mid way through my course of chemotherapy and because Steve had a streaming cold he had taken himself off to the spare bedroom rather than risk infecting me. I was unable to sleep through worry and, deciding to read for a while, I turned on my bedside lamp. At about 1.30 am I lay down and felt I may be able to nod off – I would leave my light on for once as a comfort. I had just settled myself down when I felt the bottom of my bed dip down and then rise up again. I turned round thinking that maybe Steve had seen my light and come in – but no the door was still shut.

I never gave the incident much thought but a few days later I had a private sitting with medium Keith Lloyd who described my Mom saying that she came to sit on my bed the other night as I was so worried and couldn't sleep – she even said that I had decided to sleep with my light on, adding that I always had a lamp when I was little as I didn't like the dark. Likewise on the day when I received the telephone call summoning me to hospital and I knew the news would be grim, I had gone upstairs to tell Paul where we were going and the light in the computer room went on and off all on its own for several minutes plus the cursor on the computer screen was doing a little wobbly dance on the screen without anyone touching the mouse. It was Paul himself who said "This is Spirit isn't it Mom?" Several days later this was confirmed at a Church Service which Steve and I attended. The medium, who had never set foot in our Church before and did not know me from Adam, came to us with her second message describing Mom and how she had been so brave when she passed with cancer. She said that Mom had been turning the lights on and off in our house this week. It was when I related these two incidents to my surgeon that he challenged me write this book.

Maybe now you are beginning to see how spirit communication arrives in many forms to help and guide us. At the time it is not always possible to realise why they have happened, but when you look back the purpose usually becomes clear.

# The Science Of It All

This chapter has got to offer an explanation as to how and where the spirit world exists. There will be much reference to other books, particularly 'On The Edge of The Etheric' by Sir Arthur Findlay. This won't be an easy task but I have to try because 'blind acceptance' is not the way of a true spiritualist. So let's press on!

Firstly, it is absolutely impossible to understand the nature of the spirit world unless we can comprehend the true structure and functioning of this one. Spirit exits on a vibration which is many, many times faster than ours, but our world is vibrational too, albeit a much denser and slower one. This earth may seem solid to us but solid it is not. Everything on earth is made up of atoms. They are so tiny that around a million of them would fit into the full stop at the end of this sentence. Now each atom consists of a core or nucleus (made up of protons and neutrons) with a quantity of electrons spinning around it. Next, let's think carefully about the space within each atom. The distance between the nucleus and its orbiting protons is relative to the space between the sun, earth and planets in our own solar system. Just ponder on this a while, there is this relatively massive amount of space within every single atom on earth. So are we, or our world, solid? No, not by any stretch of the imagination (every science would have to agree here). We and our world are a collection of constantly vibrating and changing atoms. Physical matter is an open network of protons and electrons vibrating within atoms. The invisible ether which is now believed to be the basic substance of the universe is what connects the minute electrical charges (positive and negative) within the atom. In fact, the most solid and permanent part of you and I is our spirit. It is the earthly vibrating Mass that is now gathered around our spirit which at present forms our 'earthly overcoat'. It was Sir Arthur Findlay in his wonderful book 'On the Edge of the Etheric,' who said that if all the ether or space was removed from our physical bodies, leaving only protons, neutrons etc. then each of us would be no bigger that the end of a pencil. Bear in mind also here that every 2-7 years (it varies from cell to cell) every single cell of your body will have been replaced, so you are only the person you were seven years ago. By virtue of the spirit within, the rest of you is transient as it constantly replaces itself. The etheric body within you (the spirit which survives death and moves on) is your body's 'blue print' and holds together what is the vibrating mass of your physical body.

It is solely because of vibration that we have the concept of colour. Sir Isaac Newton discovered the true nature of colour; that all light is white but that this white light consists of the colours of the rainbow. As this white light reaches earth different surfaces absorb different colours from it's spectrum leaving only one to be reflected. For example, a blade of grass is green because grass absorbs all the other colours from the white light spectrum apart from the green one which remains on it's surface thus making it green. So you see it is not only physical matter which is vibrational but colour too not to mention sound as well. Sir Arthur Findlay uses a diagram to illustrate the variety and scope of various rays in 'On the Edge of the Etheric'. He shows that as far as rays are concerned (infra-red, ultra violet, x-rays etc) our human powers of perception are really limited. Those that we can normally perceive compared to these that we know exist "are as an inch is to a mile!" WE SENSE SO VERY LITTLE AS HUMAN BEINGS.

Now we come to the location of the spirit world. It is here, now, all around us, inter-blended with our physical world. The reason that we can't see it is that its vibrational rate is infinitely faster than our own. This is why we can't see spirit unless we are mediumistic and thus have the right 'radio receivers in our head.' This means that spirit does not recognise earthly barriers like doors and walls. It's atoms are infinitely faster than ours and can pass straight through our solid matter. So our world is solid to us because it is at the same vibrational rate as us. Likewise, the spirit world (far from being 'airy fairy') is just as solid to spirit people because they are on the same vibrational rate as it is. By the conclusions of this book, the fact that spirit is ever present and all around us is to be proved to my friends and I beyond all doubt!

So many people dismiss the idea of spirit just because they are unable to see it themselves. I'll illustrate just how short sighted this is by using the example of a 'little demo' given to us at Bromsgrove Spiritualist Church from time to time by our long standing member Alan Perry who has a life long interest in the scientific aspect of 'spiritualism'. He places a ruler with half of it's length held down on our lectern and then 'twangs' the other end and asks the congregation what they see. The answer is invariably 'nothing at all' because the bottom, airborne, half of the ruler is vibrating so fast that it is invisible to us. It is obviously there but we are no longer able to register it with our physical senses. Really, it's like watching TV isn't it? We know that 'Coronation Street' or 'Eastenders' exists because it is there on our screen, but if we stick our head out of the window and gaze up we really can't see great chunks of it whizzing through the sky can we? So, if we can be open enough to accept reality as encompassing both earthly life and spirit life we can still only acknowledge a certain percentage of it because of our own current low sense of awareness. In many respects we are at present trapped by our limited physical senses. Our body may be 'the temple of spirit' but in some ways it is very limiting, rather like having our head stuck in a cardboard box. The few holes cut into this box (i.e. our present senses) allow only glimpses of what is really out there. Our perception of reality expands once we pass to spirit and we are no longer encumbered by our 'cardboard box'.

Sir Arthur Findlay explains this sense-limitation by asking us to imagine we are seated in a church in the dark with only candles dotted about. We have never viewed this building in daylight and so to us it is only a dark space interspersed by the glow of our candles. You are not able to appreciate it fully as a church until you see it in daylight when the whole picture becomes visible. This is us on earth now peering somewhat dimly through our limited senses. It is all a matter of perspectives. Man is often very slow in this respect. Why, only a matter of four hundred years ago, man saw the earth itself as the centre of the solar system and the universe, the stars and sun were believed to revolve around us. It was only when Galileo came on the scene that we learned our true place in the solar system and now through scientific insights we realise we are an infinitesimal speck in the cosmic picture.

Joan Hodgson in her book 'Why on earth' feels that our present sense limitations are there to protect us at this stage in our development. She says our physical senses are as 'doors of protection' wisely barred until the soul is trained and ready to cope with the wider cosmic picture. We are here to learn through our physical experience before we are able to adapt to a much wider one. I would imagine that this accounts for the reason that information from the spirit world seems so limited. They cannot tell us what it is really like because of our present limited perceptions. It would be like a bird trying to explain to a fish what it's environment is like.

Now we will stop to consider a while what this 'life force' really is. Earthly matter without this vibrational force is totally useless, it cannot hold itself together, it's molecules are no longer organised and it will quite simply decay. A tree containing this life energy stands erect and strong; the same tree when it lacks this energy lies across the ground and rots away, it's molecules returning to the earth. So life is the 'organising force' in matter. Another term for this life force is 'mind'. It is mind that influences matter and this makes mind master of the universe, just as our physical body is a medium for the expression of our mind. I remember when I went to view my Nan in The Chapel of Rest prior to her funeral. Never having seen a 'dead' body before I came away with one lasting impression. It was <u>not</u> my Nan lying in that coffin but the place where she used to be.

But this life force or 'mind' when it leaves a body or a tree has to go somewhere. Albert Einstein comes into the frame here with his E = $MC^2$ theory. This tells us that energy (i.e. life force or mind) can never be lost but is simply converted into another form. For example, when water is boiled it becomes steam or when it is frozen it becomes ice. Energy has to move on as something else, just like our mind energy. When we die, it simply moves on to find it's new means of expression in etheric rather than earthly substance.

Now to the question of how similar the spirit world is to this earthly one. I would think there would be very basic similarities, we are told that there is music, art, trees and flowers and halls of learning for the improvement of our minds. As I have explained before spirit world is as solid to them as our's is to us. However, maybe in the spirit world it will require less 'physical' effort to create as matter is much finer and lighter than here. Remember that in earthly life too our life is first shaped by our thoughts. For example, think of a chair; someone had to picture this chair in their mind prior to gathering the wood and making it with their hands. Mind first generates the pattern for everything that is here, be it the construction of this chair or the greater universal mind or God force which creates mountains etc.

I'm very much hoping that we'll be able to just 'think ourselves places' in the spirit world instead of having to find our way. (Unfortunately, nature has only equipped me with a very poor sense of direction, like many women I have to read a map by rotating it to the direction I'm travelling. This has nearly caused marriage break-up on several fraught occasions!) Maybe there won't be any language barriers in spirit either, people may just recognise our thoughts.

Spiritual philosophy teaches us that there are several 'spheres' of progression in the spirit world, each interpenetrating the last and each one of a yet finer and faster vibration. Considering this, it could be that eventually thoughts will become more and more the master of the matter around us until MIND ITSELF will ultimately be in control of our surrounding. As Sir Arthur Findlay says, this may well be the ultimate goal of our existence. "As we think so shall we be."

I have to add a section here. Just as the books I require are 'falling at my feet' so too, it appears, are radio broadcasts. I switched on this morning to hear Melvyn Bragg's programme 'In our time'. The subject today was 'Quantum Physics'. Now I can't pretend for one moment that I understood all of this programme but one factor leapt out at me and as it is very pertinent to this chapter, I will do my best to explain. In our scientific understanding we have obviously now progressed beyond the neutrons, protons and electrons which I have just mentioned. It seems we are now even beyond 'quarks' (which I have heard of) and that within these quarks scientists are now studying the existence of 'photons' and 'leptons.' These minute particles have now been discovered but scientists realise that they are missing a vital ingredient, the one that causes these new particles to behave as they do. They have named this missing ingredient as 'The Hicks Factor' and the only reason they are aware of it is because it creates an energy field. They know it's there because it influences the behaviour of the tiny particles within and around it. The fact that it is invisible and is only to be detected by it's effect on surrounding particles is what is causing the scientists such a headache. They know they are missing something here but until they look to what is now termed the 'paranormal' they will not find the key. The particle organising force they are seeking is 'mind' or 'spirit'. This is the basic force that gives matter form. WHEN WILL THEY REALISE THIS? This morning they even referred to this Hicks Factor as 'The God Particle' and they were right. The answer is right under the scientist's noses and when they eventually realise this then science and spiritualism will tune together and complete their jigsaw for them. The paranormal will then cease to be termed as such and will simply become part of science.

Scientists have a real problem with things they can't see, they are handicapped by their earthly sense limitations. As I've said before it is the THINGS UNSEEN (the eternal things) which give the universe its form.

I truly believe that, in the future, man will accept the existence of the spirit world as scientific fact. All will one day see that it is all part of the same reality. As Sir Arthur Findlay predicted 'spirit manifestation will harmonise with all that is already known.'
I feel that in the future to deny the existence of the spirit realm will be as ridiculous as being a member of 'The Flat Earth Society' is today. (It actually does still exist by the way!) Thinking has to be turned around so that 'mind' is given its proper place as the central guiding force of the universe with matter, (be it earthly or etheric) being the stuff on which it acts to create absolutely everything. This is what history itself is – 'the story of the development of the human mind in relation to its surroundings.' Hence it is this mind element of the universe which we cannot see which is the most important thing of all, it is the factor which has the power to give matter both form and expression. The things we can see now are passing things, whilst those unseen are eternal.

I will draw to a close here by yet again quoting Sir Arthur Findlay from 'On the Edge of the Etheric'. If we remember that this work was written in 1932 we can see what a great forward-thinking man he was and how modern day science is still in the process of catching up with him. He wrote, "The Ether of space can now be taken as the one great unifying link between the world of matter and that of spirit."

A book which I have read during the latter part of my illness is 'The French Revelation' compiled and researched by N. Riley Heagerty. This is perhaps the only writing which surpasses Arthur Findlay's 'On the Edge of the Etheric' for me. It really lives up to its title as 'a revelation' and on the book jacket Medium Colin Fry says that it is set to become a classic of spiritual literature. I'm sure he is right, get your hands on a copy! Anyway as he discusses the chemical make up of this world and the next spheres. He says that in the spirit world, just as here, 'matter' exists as a separate substance from 'force' or 'life – force' and says that 'spirit material' is nothing more that earthly matter raised to a higher degree of activity. So in both existences we have matter and life force. The physical world is a counterpart of the spirit world. Heagerty's book (much of it directly sent from spirit) talks of a constant refinement of matter particles which move up through the spiritual spheres - the denser or graver staying earth bound whilst refined particles speed up and move upwards for use in spiritual spheres. Interesting this, in other words the spiritual world functions temporarily through matter, just like our own earth does. Science will gradually come to realise that this manipulation of matter by life force is a constantly repeated and refining process as vibrations speed up throughout the universe.

# Bits and Bobs

Our attitude to material wealth can speak volumes about us. We obviously all need to attain a certain standard of living for the ease and comfort of our physical bodies but to get too wrapped up in the material trappings of this life would seem to be a wasted effort. After all we all have to move on eventually and leave it behind us – 'there are no pockets in shrouds'. It is not what we have but what we do with it that counts. Being really wealthy could be a help to your spiritual education if you are capable of creating the right balance between your own needs and using it unselfishly for the betterment of those around you but progression can be hindered if money becomes a greedy obsession. As M.H. Tester states in his book 'How to be Healthy, Wealthy and Wise' "Money is a means to an end. You should not get lost in the fascination of the means". Winning that vast sum on the lottery may be some people's dream but it could just as easily turn into a nightmare; maybe altering your relationship with family and friends and bringing with it a great responsibility – some folks just couldn't cope with it. My Great Uncle Hubert used to say to me when I was little: "Shirley what you want and what you need are two entirely different things" and he was so right. We should look upon money as a means of getting around this earthly plane whilst doing our best by others. I have always tried not to spoil my son Paul and sometimes with just the one offspring this proves quite difficult. But a child who has had every whim catered for is never going to appreciate and value things. It is important to leave them something to strive for – it is not good for us to have everything we desire handed over on a plate.

How often have you heard it said, "We come into this life with nothing and we go out of it with nothing". Whilst this is undoubtedly true materially, spiritually we can take an awful lot with us if we heed our lessons along life's way. This is where money may well have helped us if we have used it wisely to benefit others and not just ourselves.

When we take the global view here things may seem to have gone really awry. Half the world starves whilst the other half is sated with food and doesn't know what to do with it's wine lakes and butter mountains. This shows that we are not heeding our second Spiritualist principle 'The Brotherhood of Man'. I just hate waste. Full stop. All too frequently you can eat out and the people on the next table have just 'picked at' their food and left most of it. Why did they order it if they aren't hungry? These silly people usually buy their little children huge pub meals letting them think that if is quite acceptable to eat just a quarter of it and throw the rest away-they will turn out just the same, as they will know no better. When we go out to eat every last sprig of cress and wedge of lemon is snaffled up! I can't be doing with waste.

But paradoxically, those people who have barely enough to subsist on may just have more in their 'Spiritual Bank Account' than we in the West. The pace of life is often slower and less frantic here leaving people more time to communicate with and care for one another and the planet. The extended family is often still part of life's pattern in these poorer countries whereas here people often live miles from their own kin and hardly have time to say hello to their next-door-neighbour as they whiz to and from work. So in a spiritual sense who is the poorer? In order to make a positive difference to our planet we have to use resources well and cut down on waste and pollution. This responsibility is collective but it starts with each one of us – we must all do our bit.

Always remember too that even if you do not have enough monetary wealth to share with your fellow man there is one commodity of great value that can be shared and that is time. To spend time and give of your own self to someone is often the greatest gift. Even with material gifts it is not always what we spend that counts but the time and trouble we have taken to select the present. I always appreciate a small carefully chosen card more highly than a big glossy chocolate-box affair.

Aside from the spiritual wealth which we do take with us when we pass over, let's switch our attention to what it is that we can leave behind us here when we go. Well, the first thing that comes to mind is the example we may have set. I still try, every day, to live up to the example left to me by my Mom and Dad. They had so many qualities worth emulating and I hope I have mirrored them in some ways. Secondly, in a more concrete sense we might have built up a business which we have handed down to our offspring which will continue to provide employment when we have gone. The third thing we can leave is our advice to others. My family have left me with many a wise motto which I do call upon when necessary. Aunty Annie used to say: - "Things don't just happen. You have to make them happen." *(a really good motivator this one)*. Uncle Hubert's favourite was "Always cut your coat according to your cloth" *(living within your means is a truly sound approach amidst life's material temptations)*. Advice from my Mother-in-law, Connie was "least said soonest mended" *(How true – it often pays to hold your tongue during an argument – damage by words very often proving irreparable)*. And finally we come to my Mom's favourite, the one that has proved so true since losing her: - "When one door closes another one opens".

Perhaps we should include the quality of vanity here, as it is a part of our material world. I think we are all guilty of this to a certain degree. I know that my recent hair loss due to 'chemo' has really bothered me. Although I've managed to hang onto about a third of my previously rather thick mop, I am now getting friends to inspect the crown of my head daily for signs of tiny hairs sprouting and I can't wait to have a decent 'hair-do' again. But as our bodies are merely earthly overcoats there is no mileage in bothering too much about them as long as you keep them healthy. Cherish your health because, believe me, it is your greatest worldly asset. Lines and wrinkles should be accepted with grace, as they are as natural as the

Autumn leaves and give character to us all as we age. Let's just be grateful that old age doesn't come suddenly upon us overnight. Just imagine, you went to bed young and beautiful and wake up to find that everything has either sagged, wrinkled, changed colour or, worse still, dropped off altogether! But, joking apart, it is the beauty on the inside which is important. The body will some day be discarded and will return to the dust from whence it came. It is just the car you are driving for the time being.

The talents and abilities which we all have in different form and measure are something else we can share. We can pass on skills to those younger than us so that they will not be lost. As I've said before, creative energy flows so much better when you have a good and selfless outlet for it!

So be diligent about material wealth. Take stock of what you've got, enjoy it and count your blessings. Most importantly share it whilst you can. Ensure that the effort you expend is in the spiritually profitable areas and don't work yourself into a frenzy acquiring possessions which you will have to leave behind you in the end. I will quote M.H. Tester again here- "To limit your desire is maturity". Attitude to material life is one of the reasons that a true knowledge of the next spheres of life is essential. If Man remains ignorant of it throughout his earthly sojourn how can he use his resources wisely? It is just so vital to know that life on earth is a mere speck in your whole existence but that it is also a very important part of your preparation. In his book 'The French Revelation,' N. Riley Heagerty bemoans the fact that such a small proportion of Mankind has proper knowledge of the afterlife that: - "The many go out into the great beyond, paupers".

Lets tie up this chapter by quoting from Charles Dickens' wonderful work 'A Christmas Carol', *(my favourite story which I watch or read without fail every Christmas)*. Marley's ghost, heavily laden with "the chains he forged in life," laments his wasted earthly life of materialism and sees, now too late, how his lifespan should have been spent.  He wails: -"Business, business, Mankind was my business" – **LET'S MAKE SURE THAT IT IS OUR'S TOO!**

# What Makes A Medium

Let's start with the technical definition of a Medium here as 'A person through whom communication can be held with the spirit world.' Mediums are not fortune tellers, their job in a Spiritualist Church is to prove that life is eternal. Sometimes *(it can't be denied)* they do see the fuller picture of your life, as did the first one I consulted which I mentioned in an earlier chapter. It has been my experience over the last twelve years that Mediums are usually very loving and giving by nature. They do not get paid for coming to our services, only claiming a modest amount for their travelling expenses. Their desire is to help people along life's pathway by comforting the bereaved and bringing through advice and reassurance from the spirit world by using their special gifts. Of course, as in every walk of life, charlatans do exist; mediumship is no exception to this.

I now have many friends and acquaintances who are Mediums and, believe me, they have often lived really tough lives and suffered a great deal of harsh blows and difficulties before their gift was either developed or given to them in the first place. This must sometimes be 'a right of passage' somehow and for a very good reason. Until we have struggled to overcome life's hardships we have probably not developed sufficient 'grit' to fulfil this role of spirit communication. Also Mediums must be able to sympathise and empathise with humanity and until they have been through some of life's troubles themselves they would not be aware of how others feel. Trouble and strife also creates a strength and resilience which is also a necessary quality for mediumship. It is definitely not for the faint hearted – standing on a public platform, sometimes facing a room full of complete strangers and just having to trust that spirit will be there to do their bit. Each demonstration of mediumship is, in essence, an experiment and if the medium did not trust in spirit it would not be possible. This blind trust is my current lesson and believe me it isn't easy!

Countless times I have listened to mediums in the back hall after services saying how gruelling a task it all is. Mediums spend years and years learning to strengthen their link with spirit. During the service perhaps just one message has truly touched the heart of a grieving relative and so they say, "This is what it is all about. This is why I do this job." On occasions these messages are life-changing; giving the strength to move on with earthly life because WE KNOW at the end of the day we will all be re-united. We still owe it to those who we have loved and temporarily lost to do our best and not let them down. My first substantial message from my Mom elated me – it was the start of a whole new wider horizon.

I would just love to have this priceless gift of Mediumship but so far the occasional *(very convincing)* glimpse is all that has come my way but certainly enough to prove the afterlife to me. In fact I always say that if I didn't believe now, after all I've been shown, then I would be 'a bit thick'. There would be just no other explanation. I would add here, *(at the risk of sounding immodest)*, that on my school-leaving report my English teacher wrote that "Shirley has a keen and analytical mind". I have used this to do my research by listening to literally hundreds of Mediums and have come to the very pleasing and positive conclusion THAT WE ARE ETERNAL BEINGS. It amazes me that there are so many highly intelligent and intellectual people who don't even give this aspect of existence headroom; really clever bods like Melvyn Bragg and Ludovik Kennedy who would seem to have looked into almost every aspect of life and its philosophy yet have missed this basic simple truth.

I suspect that some of my friends consider me 'as nutty as a fruitcake' for spending half of my life at Spiritualist Church. One or two of them believe that this life is it! – Gosh what a surprise they are in for. I always agree to differ but do make the point that I will have the last word on this matter. If I'm wrong *(which I know I am not)* then neither party will ever know and if I am right we shall all know. I think you'll agree that 'I'm on a winner' here. But someone else's proof cannot be your's on this matter. Spiritual truth has to be discovered for ourselves with, of course, the invaluable help of The Medium.

Whilst, as I've just explained, Mediums have often endured a 'toughening up' process through life experience, there is definitely no particular type of person who is likely to be mediumistic. Mediums are as diverse as life itself; all classes, creeds and occupations are included and whilst some mediums are of high intellect others would seem altogether much simpler souls. We can deduce from this that spiritual truth comes from all angles and from within all people. Sometimes a simple soul can be more aware of simple spiritual truth than someone whose head is too busy with his or her intellect. Each Medium brings their own personal qualities to a service and each time there is something new to be learned.

When we stop to consider the functioning of the communication system we call Mediumship there is so much to weigh up. Information is travelling from thinking beings in one state of vibrational life to thinking beings in a very different vibrational one. So the spirits have to slow their rate of vibration greatly in order to penetrate the really thick, dense, physical and earthly vibration. At the same time we have to try to raise and lighten the vibrations here on earth so that they can reach us. This is why we sing and encourage happiness in the service before the communication starts. The Medium is the 'link machine' for this 'meeting of the vibrations'. The difficulty is that he/she is not a mere machine but a human being whose aura, energy, mind and life experience are used by the Spirit World to impart their information. The data from Spirit is received by our Medium using various senses; Clairvoyance (seeing), clairaudience (hearing), clairsentience (feeling or 'knowing'), and even clairsmellience (receiving various scents). All of this information has to be interpreted by the Medium before being relayed to its earthly recipient. Often information if presented by way of symbols which require interpretation. Spirit will often draw on a medium's personal experiences; for instance if their Granny had a severe spinal problem then they may be presented with a vision of Granny to pass on the details of a spinal condition suffered by someone else in spirit.

To add even further to the complexity of this communication business we must remember, also, that everyone retains their personality in the Spirit World, together with it's myriad of adherent faults and idiosyncrasies and in order to communicate the spirit often needs to be able to blend with the Medium to a certain degree. My Mother, who was full of confident determination, will come through most types of Medium. My Dad, on the other hand, was generally quiet and reserved and nearly always chooses a softer, gentle medium plus he will nearly always come through at a private one-to-one sitting, but then he was a very private person. My Mom, who led me to the Church three weeks after her passing, was first in the queue and the first word I heard from the platform was her name. She had literally propelled me through those church doors and I was the first recipient of the evening to boot! My 'In Laws' were very gentle and reserved folk and they, like Dad, nearly always choose a gentler Medium or a private sitting. Very often Mom will come through first and the rest of them will follow behind, she is often the spokesperson which makes sense to me. It is also vital to realise that those who have gone on ahead of us to spirit are still basically the same as they were here, so advice they give to us is still only to be taken as their opinion or the way they see things. They are not all-knowing at this stage in their development.

Mediumistic technique is also a very personal matter. Mediums all have their own way of working. Some are fortunate enough to see a light over their recipient and can then zoom straight in, *(Doris Stokes was one of these),* but others can often wrestle with establishing their link. If two or three of the congregation can take, say, 'Derek' they then have to narrow it down by giving snippets of evidence, for instance: "This Derek, who I have here, liked fishing". It is only on rare occasions that an earthly link cannot be established. It is always important to be very honest with a Medium. Believe me, it is no use at all saying 'yes' when you should be saying 'No,' this could be an important message for someone else. Likewise it is vital to play your part in a communication by speaking up if you can perhaps take all the forthcoming information when the person being spoken to cannot. Lines can become crossed in this complicated process and Mediums, as I've stressed before, are only human like you or I. Always be honest with them and, of course, never, ever feed them with any information.

Some Mediums are capable of sustaining two or even three links at the same time, placing you 'on hold' whilst they shoot over to someone else and then returning to you to finish off. Sadly, the lady at our Church who was Queen of this technique passed to Spirit last year (2003). Val Smith was a real 'fountain of Mediumship'. Our President, Mel Clark, often picked her up from Stourbridge where she lived and she would invariably start giving clairvoyance to Mel the moment she got in the car and generally all the way home again too. Sandrea Mosses, who trained under Val works this way, too; some Mediumship can be so energetic! Some Mediums will view their spirit contact 'objectively' (i.e. standing besides someone's chair in the church) but generally it is received 'subjectively' i.e. within the Medium's head.

There are a host of personal qualities which are required by Mediums. Tact and diplomacy are a must. Sometimes personal information is given to them and the message must then be 'wrapped up' so that only the recipient knows what is being said. Often on these occasions a Medium will offer to continue the contact after the service in private. On other occasions the Spirit communicator may be using language of the more colourful variety and this has to be 'toned down' to platform standard. After all, if Uncle Sid 'swore like a trooper' when he was here chances are he is still doing it over there, one thing he won't be doing is floating around on a little fluffy cloud playing a harp! I really can't be doing with this *'Rest in Peace'* stuff. I reckon that we will have just as much to do over in Spirit as we have here – I hope so anyway!

The virtue of patience is all too often necessary for the Medium too. It often takes years to develop to platform standard and when they finally come to work on the rostrum they still have to learn to cope with a congregation. The energy produced by the people forms an important part of the condition they have to work in. Positive loving energy is needed and to be faced by a glum looking individual with arms crossed and that 'Go on prove it to me' look set fast on their face, is at best unhelpful and at worst impossible. A Medium requires the energy within the room to be speeded up in order for spirit to be able to slow down enough to reach our earthly vibration. This is where music helps in raising the vibes. Many folk will merely grunt in response or worse still just nod or shake their head. Here again, the voice vibration is essential for the Medium to both confirm and encourage the link. If he/she is conversing with someone on the back row and they just nod or shake their head it is very boring for the rest of the congregation in front who are hearing no response and therefore don't know if the Medium is any good or not. I would say that those on the other side of life are the liveliest party sometimes. Men are generally the worst recipients in my experience. They take a lot of convincing, can't remember anniversary dates or family names and have often, I suspect, been dragged along to keep the wife happy.

Mediumship at its very best is always a real privilege to behold. I remember having a private sitting with international Medium, Simon James at Stansted Hall in Essex. It was quite literally like being sat in the room and having a cosy private chat with my Mom – it was the best £15 I have ever spent. Any of you who watched Spirit Medium, Gordon Smith on T.V. recently will, I think, have been similarly impressed. The crème de la crème of Mediums can take your breath away with admiration.

But the quality of prime importance for Mediumship is that of that everlasting, inter-dimensional quality: **LOVE,** which, as medium Jean Kelford, always tells us stands for '**LIGHT OF VIBRATION ETERNITY'**. A Medium must have a basic love for their fellow man. They must really take to heart our second Spiritualist principal, 'The Brotherhood of Man,' which creates sensitivity to the feelings of others and a natural desire to help and be of service.

Mediumship is perhaps the most difficult task anyone could choose to tackle. Always be prepared to give one a second chance. We all have our off days and the very nature of the information from the Spirit realms is often extremely puzzling in its presentation and hard to interpret. Conditions for communication play an important part in the Medium's demonstration and that is often out of their control. All in all, we have to conclude that a Medium's lot is far from easy, although it can be exceptionally rewarding on occasions. **GOD BLESS 'EM ALL, I SAY.**

# Exit Dad

When I lost Dad on 26<sup>th</sup> January 1998 to Spirit aged 75, I coped a great deal better than with losing Mom. The event was viewed from a totally different perspective now that I had gleaned my spiritual knowledge. This is one of the reasons that Man ought to know about the afterlife; it gives great strength and greatly affects his behaviour whilst on the earth plane. I feel strongly that the orthodoxy has had much to answer for in trying to keep a hold over the common masses. Often they tell them that communication with spirit is evil simply to hide from them the great power that ordinary mortals have over their own destiny in the afterlife, thus holding on to a great power and monopoly. It is Man's birthright to know what happens after we die. We should not have to rely on stories passed down to suit other people's religious doctrines. It is as much our right to know what happens after so-called death as it is to know that the earth is round and that we orbit the sun! It is a good thing that Man is finally waking up a little and using his own intelligence over this matter. People need to investigate for themselves. The real truth will give a purpose to earthly life that nothing else can. Anyway, off my soap box now, and back to losing Dad. I even gave him a good talking to regarding making the effort to communicate with me from spirit. He was quite 'laid back' in many respects and whereas Mom was 'champing at the bit' to get through I did have my doubts about Dad. But he promised he would be in touch and has now done so on so many occasions that I have lost count. Dad certainly seemed to be 'spiritually content' during his last weeks and said he was never alone when I left him. This was indeed confirmed in an address at Bromsgrove Spiritualist Church a fortnight or so before he passed. It was about how we are met and taken to spirit by loved ones and it certainly stopped me worrying so much about him being on his own.

The first spirit communication from Dad took place in his 'potting shed' in the garden with the aid of my good friend, medium Janet

Grainger. Now it might seem a bit odd but the reason for the strange venue was the fact that I had forgotten to bring the key to Dad's house with me. Jan and I had been to Church and she felt that she might well be able to make some contact for me. We stopped off at Dad's house which was now cleared and ready to be vacated. Anyway, the mediumship Janet managed as we sat there on an old table in the dark amidst the flowerpots was really splendid. Her first link was not with Dad but my Grandad and Jan's description of him with his "Exceptionally pale blue eyes and translucent skin" was 'spot on'. She even reminded me of how he used to almost lie back in his arm chair with his legs reaching right across the hearthrug and that he read the broadsheet newspapers which he always opened out fully, arms stretched wide. This was exactly his posture. He took up so much space that Nan and I were always 'tripping over' him. Jan also saw him with his pipe that he smoked. The way she saw Dad, as well, was very detailed saying his eyes were also blue but much darker than Grandad's and that, as he aged, "two little pouches" of skin, *as she put it,* hung beneath his eyes. Dad thanked me for looking after him. It was only me that kept him going, he said. Jan captured the essence of him, saying that he was indeed 'laid back' but always thought a lot before he spoke. She described him as a wise man and a peacemaker. He was. The symbol which Jan gave me from Dad as the contact ended, was that of a 'green bow'. It signified, she said, the bond of love between us, and now, even though it has become untied, there would always be that link, with Dad on one end of the ribbon and me on the other. It would never be broken she said. The week following this contact with spirit I was out shopping and something 'drew me' to a crystal display in a jeweller's window. My eye came to rest on a lovely crystal butterfly. I acted on impulse, went into the shop, and bought it for Jan as a special Thankyou. She was thrilled with it and told me that the butterfly holds a special spiritual significance for her as a symbol of freedom which she sometimes sees clairvoyantly. Also the make of the crystal was "Schwartz" and I had no idea that she collected Schwartz crystal. I reckon that Dad inspired me to buy this for her. He would have been as grateful for that link as I was.

The main quality that I miss about Dad is his silly sense of humour. We laughed at the same things. I will digress from spiritual matters here to relate an amusing domestic incident. It was one Summer's day after Mom's passing when I went to 'help' him. After pressing on with my usual chores, I noticed how grubby his lounge curtains were becoming. Tasks such as this had taken a back seat after Mom went. "Its such a lovely, blowy day Dad, how about flinging these curtains in the washer?" "I don't know if you *can* wash them, chick," was his reply. I searched for a fabric care label in vain. "Oh, they'll be fine Dad. I'll do them on a 'cool delicate'. No problem". As the curtains whizzed round in the washer Dad made coffee and we sat in the lounge. There was a lull in the conversation when we noticed a rather 'wet, slopping' noise. Sticking our heads around the door we found the kitchen awash with soap suds. The washer waste pipe had popped out of its bracket in the cupboard under the sink and the water had turned the kitchen into a paddling pool. We scurried around rescuing what we could; putting chairs etc. up onto the table and eventually we managed to get it all mopped up. I whipped the curtains out onto the clothes line and in no time at all they were dry. Dad had fetched the stepladders and I hooked his lounge curtains back onto the track. Oh, deary me! – They had shrunk dreadfully and now sadly dangled a good foot above the window ledge. It was all a total disaster. Dad laughed as he came out to wave me off that morning. "Thanks for coming chick," he said, "I really don't know how I would have managed without your help today!"

Dad's sense of humour never left him. Even when I accompanied him to the C.T. Scan department at The Alexandra Hospital, in Redditch a couple of weeks prior to his passing, he stared down at his large stomach, *now horribly distended with the cancer*, and pointed to a notice on the wall which read 'IF YOU THINK YOU COULD BE PREGNANT PLEASE INFORM THE RADIOGRAPHER BEFORE ENTERING.' He grinned at me and asked if I thought that could be his problem. He was trying to make me laugh even then.

Dad was always a great support to me in everything I undertook. Sometimes I have felt his presence during difficult times. The first time I went to hospital for chemo I was absolutely dreading it; indeed I was more worried than when I went in for my breast operation. I put my hand in my coat pocket only to find a photo of Dad. I remember having shown this to a friend a few weeks ago but had no idea it was in my pocket and I had selected this jacket at random from a cloakroom full before coming out. Maybe this was mere coincidence but I really felt that Dad was accompanying me to my hospital appointment just as I had kept him company for all of his.

Fifteen months after Dad's passing I was to have a wonderful contact with him. I had been down to our Spiritualist College, Stansted Hall in Essex for a week long course. Whenever you have been to the hall it always takes a few days to 'come back down to earth' as it were. A week of continuous meditation, demonstrations of mediumship and spiritual classes with no contact whatsoever with the outside world had put me into an extremely relaxed and serene frame of mind. I feel that it is probably this state of mind which made me so open to spirit when this event occurred. It was the day following my return from Stansted Hall and I was all alone simply putting away laundry in my bedroom. I turned to reach my chest of drawers and there was my Dad. He was solid and smiling and looked really well. He only remained there for five or six seconds but he was so clear and solid to me and somehow occupied a space betwixt my head and the space outside. It wasn't just seeing him so clearly that made the impact on me but the feeling of love he brought with him. It affected me physically, I felt that my heart centre would burst with it. I telephoned Ann Taylor yet again: - "Now you know what it feels like to be touched by Spirit," she said.

I will mention here a lovely piece of evidence I received at Wadebridge Spiritualist Church whilst on holiday. One advantage of having loved ones in Spirit is that they are just as likely to be with you wherever you are. The Medium described Dad to me and mentioned that I had kept an old cardigan of his as comfort. Yes, this was true. It is an old, tatty, blue one which I still keep draped over the back of the chair in my craft room and I do indeed place it around my shoulders on occasions for comfort.

When Mom went she was leaving the rest of us but when Dad went he was 'going to be with Mom.' It wasn't so hard to accept but I do miss him still. Dad and I were so at ease with each other sharing no end of laughter and content to 'just be in each other's company.'

# Annis Horribilis

In 1995 Her Majesty the Queen referred to her "Annis Horribilis" during her Christmas speech. Steve and I had our own version during 1997/8.

During the four years since Mom's passing life had jogged along. We had learned to work around the gaping hole she had left. Dad pottered on and did well looking after himself, always being positive and cheerful, on the outside anyway. Steve's parents were, however, beginning to struggle. They were both over 80 now. We would go and help with gardening and lawn trimming. We would all eat out on our visits to save Connie the trouble of cooking for us.

The Autumn of 1997 dawned, (*can't pinpoint the date exactly here*), and I was to receive a very prophetic message at our Church from Medium Ted Freeth. He told me that I was in for an extremely tough spell on my pathway, likening the forthcoming trouble to a long dark tunnel, but told me that by the end of next year I would have made it through. He did, however, leave me with the symbol of a 'spiritual wheelchair'; in other words the Spirit world would lend me their support. I informed Steve of this warning on returning home.

Around two months later, in early November, we received a very anxious early morning phone call from Steve's dad, Charles. Connie had fallen at home and was in pain and unable to move. He told Steve that he had called for an ambulance and we were soon on our way to join them. We found Connie, still in great discomfort, in the casualty department of Heartlands Hospital. X-rays were taken and although there was only a hair-line crack showing on her hip, a bed was found for her on the ward. She was to remain here for several days, during which time we all ensured that she was visited every afternoon and evening. However, Charles was looking strained and becoming breathless with all the upset and effort. Towards the end of this week of hospitalisation Connie tried to get up from her bed unaided, fell and completely broke her hip. She would now have to undergo a full hip replacement.

It was during this first worry that I noticed my Dad was looking unwell. He had an unhealthy pallor about him and I noticed that although he still displayed his 'big tum' his arms and the rest of him were decidedly thinner. I kept enquiring about his health and his stoic reply was always "Well, I'm getting older now Shirl, you have to expect these things". When my cousin Gaynor telephoned to ask me "What on earth is wrong with Uncle Pete he looks awful", I decided to visit our G.P., Dr. Fernell, and discuss my worries with him. He told me that he had to see Dad. I would have to persuade him to go.

Connie had her hip replacement, was transferred to Solihull Hospital and it seemed, at first, that her operation had been successful. Charles, however, was struggling with increasing lack of breath. An appointment was made for him, also at Solihull Hospital, to see a chest specialist.

Dad was at first rather annoyed at me speaking to the doctor behind his back as it were, but I think he knew he was really ill and I had now noticed that he was buying Paracetamol tablets each time we shopped together. I transported him to see Dr. Fernell about two weeks before Christmas 1997. Tests were taken and the outcome was grim. Dad was in the advanced stages of oesophagus cancer. He was adamant that he did not want to be, as he put it, "messed around with". His way of looking at it was 'winding down' from earthly life and one thing he didn't want was a fuss. Morphine was prescribed and I told him that I would do my utmost to keep him at home and care for him. This is what he wanted – just to be at home. Dr. Fernell was wonderful, I remember he phoned me the day following the diagnosis just to ask how I was. His help throughout was to be first rate.

The ensuing few weeks were hard work and truly 'grotty'. Steve was still working at this time although he had applied for a redundancy package from B.T. Paul was really good but ten year-olds are always demanding and it must have been tough for him, the only adored grandchild on both sides, he had now already lost one grandparent and the other three were failing rapidly. I spent part of each day at Dad's house helping with housework and keeping him company. We did a lot of talking together at this time, openly discussing the spirit world, with me telling him that I would expect communications from him. He would have to make the effort to get in touch with me from the other side and he didn't let me down on this one, Bless him! Dad's medication had to be sorted and his food for the day as he was 'losing his grip' rapidly by now. At the same time Charles was becoming more and more breathless and not really coping. We asked him to come and live with us for a while but he declined, clinging fast to his independence. I would 'plate-up' dinners for him and Steve would drop them over to Solihull most nights before taking him so see Connie. Amidst all this mayhem we felt obliged to recognise that it was Christmas, for Paul's sake. I recall Paul draping a set of fairy lights around his Grandad Peter's wardrobe. By now Dad had moved downstairs into what had been Nan's self-contained bed-sitting room.

By the beginning of January I hated leaving Dad at night but he would not come to us and I remember him saying that he was never alone when I'd gone – there would be Mom amongst others from spirit drawing close to him. He was definitely 'Tuning in to Spirit' now. The consultant called to see Dad at home as he was not well enough to make the short journey to hospital. By now the gullet was closing and even soft foods would not go down. He persuaded Dad that life could be made more comfortable by the insertion of a stent to keep his gullet open, so Dad agreed. I was to take him into The Alexandra Hospital the following week. All this time I was having to keep visitors away from him – he didn't want any fuss.

We were very worried, too, about Connie now; she was not recovering from her operation and did not show the inclination to eat; it was as though she was giving up, much to Steve's distress. One night we were woken by the telephone. The hospital thought Connie was about to pass so Steve rushed in. He sat through the night with her but by morning, to everyone's amazement, she had rallied and brightened considerably. Luckily, it had been a false alarm.

On the morning when I was to take Dad to hospital for his operation I arrived to find him in what can only be described as 'a state'. The morphine dose was by now quite high and he had fallen, knocking vases, clothes and medicines all over the floor. He had lost his usual air of calm and was upset and angry, not even remembering his planned trip to hospital. I phoned The Alexandra Hospital and they sent an ambulance to collect him. I shall never forget the horror of this trip. The hospital visit was supposed to be a short stay for a little op, but he was never to return home again.

Each afternoon now meant a trip to 'The Alex.' (Steve was still at work) and then taking Charles to visit Connie every evening. I don't think I would have managed all of this had it not been for the kindness of friends, relatives and neighbours, particularly Gill my good friend opposite who often had Paul for me. It was still my intention, and Dad's, for him to come home again and arrangements were made for district nurses to come in and help. However, on the morning scheduled for his stent operation, the ward sister phoned me at home – "Shirley, your father has taken a turn for the worse, please come in". He was indeed in a bad state and had been transferred to a side ward. He wasn't fully conscious and I agreed it didn't seem right to move him home. I was then asked if I would see the doctor in order to sign a consent for him to have an operation. Somewhat puzzled I was taken to see the consultant and said that I thought it was obviously too late now for the insertion of a stent. The Doctor said yes but they needed to insert a gastroscope as they hadn't formally diagnosed his condition yet. I saw red and informed her in no uncertain terms that HE WAS NOT TO BE MESSED AROUND WITH JUST TO PROVIDE THEM WITH A DIAGNOSIS when it was obvious even to me that he wouldn't last more than two or three days. I could not believe that this had even been suggested – it defied all sense of decency.

In mid January Charles went to Solihull Hospital as an outpatient for his chest x-ray. An ambulance picked him up as by this time walking was becoming difficult through his breathlessness. The X-ray was taken and he was then pushed in a wheelchair to see Connie on the floor above. After this the hospital had sent him home in an ambulance and for some unimaginable reason, considering his state of health, had not seen him in through his door but left him at the bottom of his driveway. Around 6.00 pm that evening I received a distraught telephone call from Elsie, Charles' next-door neighbour. Charles had never reached his front door but collapsed on the driveway and Elsie had dialled 999. The paramedics arrived and whizzed him straight back to Solihull Hospital. I telephoned Steve on his mobile; he was just on his way to pick up his Dad, who he thought would be at his bungalow, to take him to visit Connie. I had to tell him to about turn and go to the hospital as now his Dad was a patient there as well as his Mom!

As you might imagine the ensuing few days were pretty horrendous. Steve at one hospital and me at the other. I would add here that we are both only children so everything was our responsibility but at least there was nobody else to argue with! A couple of days after Charles was admitted Connie's consultant called us in to explain that her body had rejected the new hip and the whole operation had to be repeated. She only had a 50% chance of surviving the surgery as, due to eating poorly, she was so much weaker now than before.

On Thursday 22nd January Steve and I both set off to our respective hospitals. My Dad was barely conscious at all but I sat and held his hand for as long as I could. On returning home I noticed that although it was not late our house was in total darkness. I went over to Gill's where my Paul was safely tucked up in bed. Apparently Steve had returned home from hospital only to be called straight back again as Charles was about to pass. He returned home at about 2.30 am. His Dad had died around 01.30 on Friday morning. We decided, together with the medical staff, that Connie should not be told until after her life-threatening operation. So began the conspiracy to keep Charles' death from her.

My Dad struggled on over this week-end. I even slept at the hospital one night in an adjoining room. At one point I became very unhappy about the level of his pain relief as Dad was groaning. Each noise he made tugged at my heartstrings. I telephoned our G.P., Dr. Fernell as it had been his promise that there would be no pain. He was great as usual, contacting the hospital and demanding that they double the morphine dose. I have to admit here that it did even cross my mind to fiddle with his morphine driver myself. I could see how its output was controlled by a screw. When you love someone it's amazing what you are driven to. Wouldn't it be great if, when you reached that point where you really felt that you must pass to the next life, you could just hop on a bus with 'Spirit World' on the front and wave everybody goodbye with a 'See you Later'. I have joked with Steve about having me put down but he said "No chance – it cost £25 to have our hamster 'Bubble' dispatched!" Steve was with me as much as he possibly could have been over this week-end, between sorting out Charles' death certificate and collecting his personal effects from hospital not to mention visiting his Mom.

On Sunday 25$^{th}$ January I was with Dad from noon onwards. Steve came and then went as there was obviously still Paul to be cared for. I thought that Dad was going to 'hang on' for ever. The sister was so kind when I said that I wished he would go now – he had suffered enough. She said that it might help if I actually gave him my permission to go. She felt he was clinging on for my sake. So I did. I said that whereas I loved him so very much, it was time to cross over to join Mom – that it was just fine by me and that I understood. He was very peaceful after this until evening when nurses disturbed him to turn him. I could not see the point of this – he certainly wasn't going to be around long enough to develop bed sores. After his 'turning' he began to cry out in pain and I begged for more morphine which was, after many tears, administered. I had reached an all time low by now and, as though sensing my distress from afar, Gill arrived saying that she thought I might like some company, *(strange how true need is fulfilled at times like this)*. Gill and I left the hospital at 10.30 pm. Early the following morning of January 26$^{th}$, the hospital telephoned to inform me that Dad had passed.

Monday morning was spent chasing death certificates etc. During the afternoon we visited Connie. Now this was going to be a tricky situation. We now had two deaths to conceal from her instead of one. We decided that we would both stay by her bedside so that each would know what the other had said to her – it would be safer this way. It was during this visit that a degree of humour stepped into our dire situation. Connie was quite chatty – ironically it was one of her better days. As we sat with our chairs drawn up to her bedside we were provided with a welcome cup of tea and were doing our best to keep the conversation light and chatty despite how we felt. Steve had just taken a gulp of tea when his Mom innocently began enquiring after my Dad's health. "Is your Dad comfortable, Shirley?" she asked "Oh yes," I replied, "He's really comfortable now Connie" *(Well The Chapel of Rest is, isn't it?)* This remark was just too much for Steve who nearly spluttered his tea all over the place! Humour is a priceless element of life and I know who would have found this the most hilarious – my Dad himself.

The same week as Charles and Pete had passed Connie successfully came round from her second hip operation. We then had the sad task of informing her that both her husband and my Dad had departed this life. She was so brave – God Bless Her!

We decided that it would be practical to have a double funeral for Dad and Charles. They got on well and Steve and I had lots of mutual friends who would want to support us at both services. There was just no point in going through two funerals when one would do. The day passed successfully – Spirit were buoying me up from inside and I coped well. After all, coping was fast becoming a way of life. In any given situation you can either choose to sink or swim. I afterwards learned that one of my aunties had remarked to the other "Isn't Shirley brave" – Aunty Maureen replied "Well she's a Spiritualist – they're different you know!" - **YES AND I'M VERY PROUD TO BE SO!** Sadly Connie could not attend her own husband's funeral so arrangements were made for the hospital chaplain to stay with her at this time and Steve taped the Service which was played to her the day after. It was the best we could do for her.

Connie struggled on in hospital for the next three months. Needless to say we kept up the visits with help from Steve's cousin, Robert, and also from Connie's life-long friend, Dorothy, a wonderful little person; totally blind and nearly 90. She used to get a taxi to hospital all the way from Sparkhill, Birmingham and we would arrange for her to be met in the hospital foyer and escorted up to see Connie *(aren't some folk just wonderful)*. However, by April, pressure was obviously on for Connie to leave hospital – she had been there for over 5 months after all. The problem was that she would need nursing care as she was unable to even turn over in bed unaided and now had bedsores too. Steve and I began a long stint of visiting and checking out various nursing homes, a very sad eye-opener this. We finally settled on St. Johns Court in Bromsgrove where she would be near to us. *(We knew that here she would be visited often as one or other of us went into Bromsgrove several times a week anyway. This was, however, regarded as a selfish act by at least one of the hospital staff and, I suspect, by the hospital social worker who had expected Mom to go to a home on 'her list' of vacant beds locally. – Steve Bach)* Sadly Connie only lasted a week in their care. She passed on 7<sup>th</sup> May, 1998, on Steve's 50<sup>th</sup> Birthday. It was also the day he received his redundancy notice from BT. Steve and I were with Connie when she passed. She wasn't hanging about. I'm sure, she wanted to go to Charles. Later, sorting through documents, we discovered that 7<sup>th</sup> May was also the date on which Connie's Father, Walter, had taken his transition to spirit.

The remainder of our 'Annis Horribilis' was one long round of house-clearing and sorting out documentation. Ted Freeth had been so right – the last document was signed during November, 1998. By the end of the year it was all done and dusted. That forewarning from Spirit was definitely of help to me. I had been both prepared for a rough time and been given the reassurance that I would cope with it all. It was a great loss to Steve, Paul and I; we are now sadly lacking in relatives. Never mind, as my Mom used to say, "You can choose your friends Shirley but you can't choose your relations" and we certainly do have some great friends.

# Peering Through The Glass

This chapter is being added to my original synopsis. It is impromptu because the idea has come from Spirit and not from me. I am simply doing as I've been told with this one. Jan Higgins passed the order on after giving me another very powerful healing session on Monday night. The subject or basic idea has been pin-pointed for me. I now have to put 'some flesh on the bones' as it were.

As I've told you before the Spirit World is not elsewhere but here and all around us. It interpenetrates our world. Spirit have suggested that it is like them peering through security glass at us. This glass is one way, like the type used for identification parades where you can see the criminal line up but they are unable to see you. Mediums have a regular 'window' which they can peer through by lowering their rate of vibration but we, on earth, are either completely in the dark or are given the occasional very exciting glimpse through a peep hole in this veil, as I have been. We are not designed, as human beings, to see them physically because of the limitations of our senses, as I have discussed in a previous chapter. It wouldn't be all that beneficial to humanity if this veil were completely transparent. Life would be too easy, we are here to learn lessons so that we may grow. These sense limitations make it all the more of a struggle and therefore more of an achievement. I mean it's very character forming, this 'life business,' isn't it?

However, living with 'the great unseen' can be of benefit, particularly by widening our perspectives and making us see how important our development on the earth plane is as a preparation for something else. The key to unison between these two 'sides of the glass' is the blending of energies. I have said before, when I glance back I can see how my physical life has been guided in a very rudimentary way by spiritual insight. We can receive advice openly and directly from Spirit through a medium but subtler help is there to be perceived by all of us if we are only open to it. We can then register certain energies from the other side of this glass.

It is in times of great need within life that we are often more able to feel the close proximity of Spirit. Their desire to help is strong when we are in distress. Recall here how my Mom turned the lights on and off and tampered with the computer when I received that grim phone call from hospital. But usually help is not quite as tangible as this but comes as an energy. This type of help has been forthcoming for me on a number of occasions. The one that stands out in my mind is the day I accompanied my Dad for his C.T. scan just prior to his passing. We had done our best to chat and even joke as we waited but the moment he disappeared through those double doors into the scanner room I experienced a feeling of utter despair. It was as though those closing doors symbolised his being taken from me – I had lost Mom and now Dad would go too. As soon as I had registered this awful moment I 'just knew' that someone or even something had come to be at my side. It was a 'presence' which surged physically through me, uplifting me and giving me strength. I felt its progress in what I can only term a physical manner from my feet upwards. It was the same 'surge of power' which I described to you when I had chickenpox and was soaking in my bath.

I feel that sometimes help via 'the blending of energies', in similar times of need, is also sent when we are in sleep state. It has happened to me on several occasions, the latest being after my recent diagnosis when I awoke one morning and 'just knew' that something, I know not what, had taken place. I felt so strong inside and my outlook had changed, I will tell you more about this later in the book.

Spirit will also show this close proximity to us by impinging thought energy on the minds of those around us. How many times have you been in dire need and a friend 'just turns up' at that moment when you felt you couldn't cope any longer. Remember Gill who 'just turned up' at hospital on the night my Dad passed? A lot of this impinging on the minds of those around me has been coming into play during my present 'adventure'. Otherwise the puzzle would never have come together.

Thoughts can obviously travel through this 'security glass' too. Remember here the silent prayer I sent out when Mom was ill which was returned to me 'verbatim' from Spirit. When my own spirit is deeply troubled I light a candle, sit quietly and send my thoughts and questions out to the Spirit World. This process is very soothing and I have learned from experience that Spirit does listen and does indeed send help, if only we are able to perceive it. And be prepared, help is not always in the form we expect – there can often be a twist in the tail of spiritual matters.

The next way to illustrate how closely Spirit can interact through this 'security glass' is the way they can make us feel compelled to act in a certain way. Sometimes we might refer to this as 'acting on impulse' or 'going with our gut feeling'. I felt this compunction when I made that first visit to Bromsgrove Spiritualist Church. It was as if my Mom had literally 'propelled' me through those church doors. I HAVE FELT THE SAME COMPUNCTION TO WRITE THIS BOOK AND HAVE DONE SO SINCE. Mr. Purser first threw down the challenge. I realise now, taking into account all the notes I have made over the past twelve years and all my spiritual messages kept in date order, *(I'm not usually this organised, believe me),* that I was supposed to write all of this to share my spiritual experiences with other people.

My Dad has managed on a couple of occasions to almost 'keep me company' through this spiritual looking glass. I recall one day after his passing when I had been busy cutting his front lawn and a nut had 'pinged off' the mower. I searched every inch of that lawn and the flower beds but to no avail. I would normally have gone straight to our nearest D.I.Y store, but for some reason I set off for a local lawnmower repair man where Dad usually went. Having purchased a replacement nut I set off back to Dad's house. As I approached a junction with the main road I was given a clairvoyant vision of Dad. He was wearing his flat cap and grinning – I could even see the gap where his one tooth was missing. But what was most evidential here is that I saw him looking out of the window of his old green car. Now he had sold this green car and bought our old red Fiesta from us. I was at that moment driving this old red Fiesta again, but the car I could clearly see Dad in now was his old green Metro. I saw him so vividly and 'felt' the essence of him to such a degree that I smiled and said out loud "Hello Dad – what have you come for?" I wasn't to have to wait long before finding out that answer to this question. I turned left at this 'T' junction and then left again. I couldn't believe my eyes – there parked outside the Bromsgrove Conservative Club *(he would have approved of this) was* my Dad's old green car. I pulled in and parked and got out to make sure that I wasn't 'seeing things'. But no, there it was, nicely done up and much more polished than it had been, but the registration number was the same. Do you know, I never ever saw that car again, it was a one off sighting. I even wonder if my Dad caused that nut to fly off the mower so that he could take me to see his old car!

We are told in the Bible that our lost loved ones are 'only in the next room'. They are so close and yet usually go totally unnoticed. It is only our limited perception that stops us seeing them but we must remember that just because you can't see something doesn't mean it's not there. It is the unseen things that are eternal whilst those we *can* see, at the moment, will pass.

So to sum up we have two vastly different vibrations of energy or life, one on one side of the glass and the other on the other side of it. It is the occasional blending of these two different energies that links us with those we have loved and lost. Remember it is this life energy which is the guiding force in our universe, matter simply collects around it to create form. If we can manage to blend our energy successfully with that of Spirit we are half way to not needing a Medium at all!

# Chapter I.

Now it is time to return to the present spiral of activity and my current illness. I will describe it as a 'spiral' because this is how it still feels to me. It's like I'm being swept up and carried along by a spiritual sense of purpose.

I shall backtrack a wee bit here to Sunday 30th May, 2004 and a Sunday service at Bromsgrove Spiritualist Church *(Note: this was the day after Shirley's first visit to the doctor after finding her breast lump a day or so previously. The Saturday emergency surgery at Cornhill Surgery has since been abolished – Steve Bach)*. My friend Chris Wagg remembers the message which I received on this day and has prompted me to include it here. It was the weekend prior to my initial visit to Mr. Purser with my breast lump. I will admit, here, that I had chatted to our Medium, Sue Tomlinson, before the service and she did know of my situation. However, the message she gave to me was to be evidential, even taking this into account, especially in retrospect. She described my Dad and to prove that he had been around me of late she said that I had recently been looking at some plans and Dad was with me at the time. This was true, I was in the throws of having a new kitchen and Steve and I had sat on the settee the day before this message to check over the plans prior to units etc. being ordered. She then proceeded to itemise the points which we needed to question on this plan. The first was that there was something wrong under the window; this was correct. We couldn't make out why a narrow space had been left here. Secondly, she said that there was "a question over the electrics" - there certainly was; we believed that these were included in the initial price quoted and this was not apparent on the itemised list we had been provided with. Thirdly, Sue said to me "And X marks the spot." There had been one power point missed off the plan and I had marked this in with an 'X'. She then told me that Dad said my present problem would turn out

O.K - I remember thinking maybe it will but not until after a lot of trouble! Sue concluded by saying that I would really "take off spiritually" by October and by the following September I would be 'back on track'. Well, as you can imagine, by now 'take off' is complete and I am well and truly airborne. As to being back on track by September, 2005, we will have to wait and see as at this point everything seems to be hanging in the balance as it were. Taking the wiser perspective here, does this 'Back on Track' mean the settling into life in the Spirit realms and continuing my pathway over there? - Who knows!

I must take you forward with me now to the Church's day of private sittings on the 9th of October, 2004. I have already related my sitting with Keith Lloyd when Mom informed me that she had been to sit on my bed. However, another matter from this day must now be added otherwise an important piece of the puzzle will be missing. I had spiritual healing on this day from medium and healer Olwyn Griffiths. She took me to a quiet corner of the hall and sat me down. At this point something made me tell Olwyn about waking, one morning, feeling really energised and strong from within (a few days after being told that my cancer had returned). I hadn't mentioned this to anyone else and I certainly couldn't remember dreaming anything, only feeling great on awakening. Olwyn just said that this sounded interesting and then gave me a lovely healing session involving the visualisation of a white light. Afterwards we sat having our lunch and she showed me some lovely cards she had produced on her computer. She had purchased a digital camera which came with a computer disk for enhancing photos. Her images were absolutely fascinating. She had faded images, distorted them, inserted colours, bubbles and stars. I was really taken with them.

Now we will move forward to Saturday, the 16th October; two days after my diagnosis of liver tumours. If you recall Steve and I were now both keen to go down the alternative therapy route and had just 'known' that we would be shown where to go. During that afternoon I received a phone call from Mel Clark, our church

President. "Shirley do you remember me telling you of an Indian herbal medicine called Carctol?" I recalled her mentioning it when I was first diagnosed with breast cancer. Mel had just 'chanced' to see a programme about it on T.V. She said that she never ever watches daytime telly but something made her sit down with a cup of coffee and switch on in the middle of vacuuming. I showed immediate interest in it and Mel then spent the afternoon sifting out the information she had on Carctol. During the week she had taken her daughter, Sophie, to the doctor's and thought she would ask him his opinion. It was that if her friend was in the situation she described then "why not go for it"? At this point Mel and I phoned for an information pack on Carctol! Mel also reminded me of her successful knee operation by psychic surgeon, Stephen Turoff, some 14 years ago. Perhaps this would be another approach. As you can see things were already starting to happen.

So we started our practical 'coping' strategy, Steve's by going to visit Pete O'Connor (who plays in a band and has a recording studio) to explore the possibility of taping my organ tunes for Bromsgrove Spiritualist Church and transferring them to CD. Returning home around 4pm there was a gift bag by the front door. It contained a book entitled 'The Journey' by Brandon Bays from my dear friend Susan Sprigg, our healing leader at church. The book is the true account of an alternative therapist in America who cured herself of a cancerous tumour the size of a basketball without the aid of conventional medicine. I was soon engrossed in this, it being concerned with the mind's ability to alter negative patterns imprinted in 'cellular memories' which she believes cause cancer.

During this Saturday morning I also told Steve of my intention to telephone Olwyn Griffiths as she had promised to give me spiritual healing whenever I felt I needed it. I knew, too, that Olwyn is very knowledgeable on the subject of alternative therapies. As I was making myself a drink prior to phoning Olwyn my telephone rang. It was Chris Wagg from church, she said that medium Jan Higgins, who was giving a trance workshop, was sorry to hear of my troubles and extended an open invitation to me to pop in and see her, but I was unable to do so due to a prior commitment with Steve. I made a mental note to ring Olwyn later.

On Saturday evening Chris rang again to recount all the strange events which transpired at the end of the Jan Higgins workshop that afternoon. The group had finished at 4.30pm and Jan had kindly suggested that they all sit in a healing circle to send the energy, which had been created, to me. The dozen or so people gathered round and Chris said that the energy was really strong. After only a couple of minutes Jan went off into trance. It had not been her intention to do so but spirit had ideas of their own! The voice of Jan's main guide, a powerful Arabian Gentleman, boomed through Jan's mouth. He said "Our sister Shirley is in trouble" then went on about how orthodox medicine had reached it's limits but those in the high spirit realms had other ideas. Help would be forthcoming and I would be shown where to go and what to do. Putting modesty aside, I was, he added a special lady to them, as I had done much work for spirit. Jan 'came round' and the group ( a couple of them were quite emotional I was told) chatted over the contents of the message. Chris also told Jan that I was considering going to see Stephen Turoff, the famous psychic surgeon. Jan was immediately interested in this. Being familiar with his techniques she said she would be able to back up any work done on me by Stephen Turoff as she was familiar with the energy he uses. I remembered that I still had to ring Olwyn.

The following morning, Sunday morning, our first phone call of the day was from Chris again. She asked if I was going to church that evening. I said I hadn't even thought about it as I was still 'in a whirl' with all that was going on. She told me that (surprise, surprise) Olywn Griffiths had agreed to come to chair the service as our other chairpersons were all otherwise engaged. She added that Olwyn had worried about the music and starting off hymn. I told Chris to assure her that I would come to play the organ - Olwyn was just the person I needed to see! (This must be why I kept putting off phoning Olwyn - I didn't need to).

Sunday evening came round and something made me ask husband Steve if he would come to church with me. Now this was most unusual as, although Steve believes, a Spiritualist Church is not really his thing. He always says it is like him asking if I would like to go to the British Steam Railway Interest Group with him, but on this occasion for some reason I asked him and he said "yes". We arrived just in time for me to sort the music out then the medium came from the back hall to start. She was totally new to Bromsgrove Spiritualist Church. Her name was Christine Jackson and she had come from Walsall to serve us for the first time. Christine zoomed in on Steve and I with her second message of the evening. She had my Mother, we were given her passing with cancer and the fact that she never complained and was so brave. She then said she had been putting the lights on and off in our house that week to show us she was there. Chris continued by asking if we had noticed the footsteps on the landing at night - I replied that I hadn't but Steve interrupted me here saying "Yes, I have – twice" I got up to see if anyone was there (I now have Steve noticing spirit activity that I have missed myself!). I remembered then that Keith Lloyd had told me on Saturday, 9th October at our day of sittings that both my husband and son would soon be receiving their proof of Spirit. It was coming to fruition less than a fortnight after receiving the message. My mom then gave me the symbol of a red umbrella of protection from Spirit. She told me that I was not to be with people who were negative about my condition. Positivity would be the way forward!

Following the service Olwyn saw me and was really helpful. We chatted purposefully regarding healing and diets. She knew about this Carctol medicine and said that the lady who had introduced it to this country, Dr Rosie Daniels, worked at the Bristol Cancer Help Centre. She knew that I would have a low acid, vegetarian-type diet and that I would have to drink 6 or 8 glasses of cooled, previously boiled water each day. I then mentioned to Olwyn about the book which Susan Sprigg had left on my doorstep, 'The Journey' by Brandon Bays. She smiled, "I know quite a lot about her". Not only had she read the book but one of her friends lived next door to Brandon Bays in America!

The next day (Monday, 18th October) I was washing my hair when Steve shouted: "You've got a visitor Shirl.". I hurried down to find Steve's friend, Paschal Morris downstairs. Paschal had a major operation for bowel cancer last year and is now super fit and running miles each day as he used to – he's a real inspiration! He had brought me a book entitled 'The Bristol Approach to Living with Cancer'. This was about the Bristol Cancer Help Centre the very place that Olwyn had mentioned to me yesterday. I never had to go and buy the book, it came to me via the kindness of our neighbour, Paschal.

Now we begin to see what I meant only two days ago when I said to Steve that we would be 'pointed in the right direction'.

# Chapter 2

Today, Wednesday, 20th October 2004, I have my appointment at POWCH (Princess Of Wales Community Hospital). The information on Carctol popped through the letterbox this morning, very interesting but minus the list of UK Doctors who will prescribe it. Steve telephoned to request this missing list. Half an hour later Mel phoned. She had received her Carctol pack but, again, minus the list of Doctors. Later in the day when her computer was back she would be able to search the Internet for it. Steve and I had no luck finding it on the net either. So for now we had information on Carctol but nobody to contact. Steve suggested we show our information to Mr Purser that afternoon to see what his opinion was.

At 2pm we were sitting in Mr Purser's consulting room and we told him we were going down the alternative therapy route. "Right then", he said, "What are we going to try?" I passed over to him the sheets on Carctol. "The trouble is", I said, "It isn't licensed in the UK so UK Doctors won't prescribe it". "I'll prescribe it for you, Shirley", was his immediate reply. My astonishment must have shown on my face. "You look surprised", he said. "Well yes", I replied. "Well we haven't been able to put you right, Shirley, so what right have I to say that something else won't work for you? I'll prescribe Carctol and I'll monitor you whilst you're taking it". I left Mr Purser with a prescription for Carctol written on an NHS form. Steve and I thought it wouldn't be that easy and indeed it wasn't. We tried three chemists that afternoon but to no avail. Carctol was not available through any NHS suppliers and indeed they had never heard of it. Returning home we found a message from Mel. She had now located the missing list of UK Doctors on the Internet. She had printed it off and would come up in the morning to help. As promised, Thursday morning, Mel arrived. We decided to phone the nearest Doctor to us who was at Leicester. Mel explained my situation to Dr Kanu Patel.

Firstly, he was amazed that a consultant surgeon had agreed to prescribe Carctol. He said that he would be quite willing to co-operate with him, but that Carctol was part of Ayurvedic health and diet regime and he would need me to have a private consultation with him. A copy of my medical notes would also be required. I telephoned the hospital and related this to Mr Purser's secretary. The same afternoon she returned my call. Mr Purser would be happy to liase with Dr Patel. He had spoken to him in Leicester and my notes were already winging their way to him. This really is co-operation at it's best; I think you'll agree. I telephoned Dr Patel and made an appointment for 11am on Thursday next week, 28th October.

Mel and I had a good 'heart to heart' today. She feels caught up in this 'spiritual vortex' surrounding my illness. We both share a sense of expectancy and excitement at the moment. We are being 'ushered' very precisely by Spirit to where we are meant to be. It was strange, wasn't it, that the illusive list of UK Carctol Doctors was missing from both my information pack and from Mel's and that we were able to locate it on the net. This meant that had we had this list of Doctors before, maybe I would have gone directly to Dr Patel, thus not involving Mr Purser. Mel and I both feel that it was meant to happen this way. Maybe this herbal medicine is to be more widely used by the medical profession. Mr Purser with his open-mindedness may need to be aware for the greater good. The hospital sent away some of my cancer cells to be tested for a new antibody treatment which may help my liver. Mr Purser said this could be used at the same time as my taking Carctol, if the results are favourable.

I have just been in touch with trance medium Jan Higgins. She has been strongly directed by Spirit to give me healing so we have agreed to meet at Bromsgrove Spiritualist Church on Monday, 25th October.

Today, Sunday, 24th October, I attended our evening service at Church. I rushed in literally at the last minute and had not time to chat before it began, the reason being that I had mislaid my car keys and after a fruitless search ended up at the last minute in Steve's car. Our medium was Sue Curley who had not seen me for six months, so she wasn't aware that I even had breast cancer when she took the platform. She came to me with her second message of the evening describing my Mom and Dad and saying that Mom had passed with cancer. She then said "This makes no sense at all to me Shirley, but Mom's shouting "Tell her it's not what I had. Tell her it's not what I had". My Nan then stepped forward with a bag of herbs for me. Sue then gave me 'a Rose'. I said that Rose was my Nan's middle name but she was not satisfied with this, she felt she was getting Rose for a different reason and it was certainly not the flower. She said that my Mom was talking of losing her hair and asked me if she had lost her hair with cancer treatment. I said "no" but that I was currently on 'chemo' and my hair had gone very thin. Sue was very surprised by this and said she would have a chat with me after the service. As we talked and she caught up on my health news I mentioned it was Dr Rosie Daniels who had pioneered the use of Carctol in the UK. Sue said "Yes that's where Rose came from - it is connected to the herbs that your Nan gave you". Chris Wagg and I mulled over the latest developments and she offered to take me to Dr Patel in Leicester anytime as his practise is in Melton Road, where her dad lives.

Today is Monday 25th Oct and my friend Jan Grainger came up for a coffee. As we nattered away in the lounge she commented; "Shirl., there is such a lot of spirit energy in the room". I knew she wanted to link to Spirit but as it was half term and quite noisy in our house I suggested we take a stroll up by the reservoir at the back of my house. We sat on a bench overlooking a field of sheep and Jan tuned. Her mediumship was really good. She got my dad through and then Steve's dad describing his garden and that he had been a carpenter and he had lathes etc. in his garage at home. But then she seemed to go up on to another level and exclaimed very excitedly that she could see me now in a big opaque bubble. She described the colours as pastel and translucent and she said that all around the edge of it was a deep scarlet red giving me strength. She said that Spirit was absolutely everywhere around this bubble and that they were all supporting me. Janet then literally took my breath away when she told me that Spirit were telling her that recently they had taken me on a journey and that I had been energised and woke feeling really good. This strength she told me was coming from a higher source. It was true I had woken feeling great and much stronger in outlook. The only person I had mentioned this to had been Olwyn Griffiths on the day of sittings. Jan finished her link which had been so powerful and left her rather emotional. It was as we walked back to the house that I suddenly realised that this was to be the cover for the book. Me in this opaque bubble with the deep red energy, protecting me, all around and giving me strength. This vision summed up just how I felt at the moment, both protected and energised by the Spirit World. I knew, too, that I must ask Olwyn to create this cover with her new digital camera and put it on disc.

After Janet had left I decided to ring Olwyn whilst all this was still fresh in my mind. "Shirley, you're not going to believe this...". "Try me", I answered. By now the unbelievable was becoming the norm. She said that over the last couple of days she had been out taking photos of Autumn leaves with her new camera. She had taken four photos of a lovely red Acer in the park near her home. Returning home she put the first three photos onto her computer screen and knew immediately how she wanted to adapt them but the fourth one she had simply inserted a large bubble into the centre of the red and could go no further. She had left it, unfinished, feeling that spirit would let her know what was to go inside the bubble. Now she knew; it was me. The book cover was half done already. Olwyn also told me that she felt she had to carry out a power healing circle for me and she had been told Steve was to be the fourth healer. He will do this. Red will be the colour.

At around 2pm an old friend from church, Val Snow, rang me. She knows Jan Higgins well and Jan had told her of my present situation. She called to send her love and to tell me she would send her energy for the first healing service at 7pm that night. I chatted at length with Val regarding all the strange events and the Carctol treatment and I said to her that I feel that I am to be a Guinea Pig in some way. Partly it was because of all the coincidences and partly because I was feeling such a sense of purpose about it all. Anyway at 7pm I met Jan Higgins as arranged. The healing was very relaxing and she worked with me in three different ways, sometimes working with the aura, sometimes hands on, and finally in a manner of pointing. All the time I could feel a very warm energy passing from her to me. She also gave snippets of mediumship telling me that Mom was there and asking, "Who was it that liked The Sound of Music, I feel it is an Auntie". "Yes", I said, "Auntie Annie was mad keen on it". Apparently, she had sung a medley from the musical as Jan was healing! We arranged to meet on the next Monday to continue the healing. She followed me part of the way home as she was going to visit Val Snow and give her healing too. The following morning Val Snow phoned again, "I think I've got another snippet for your book here Shirley," she said. Apparently, when Jan Higgins had arrived at her house last night, she seemed a bit pre-occupied. Val, being her usual intuitive self, enquired what was wrong. She asked if the healing hadn't gone well with me. Jan said "yes" the healing was fine, but she told Val that before she left home she felt something was going on regarding me. Before she left home that night she had asked Spirit; "What is all this about with Shirley – what's going on here?" Her guides told her I was to be used as (and I quote) "a Guinea Pig by the spirit world". Jan had felt that she really couldn't give me that news saying; "The poor girl will be terrified" so she held it back. Val, smiling now, had put her mind at rest telling her that I was one step ahead of her here and had indeed used the very words "Guinea Pig" when we chatted on the phone earlier yesterday. This is really coming together now isn't it! I really feel now that the spirit world is using me for some end here. On one hand it would be lovely to be back in good health again but there is another facet of me that wouldn't swap places with anyone at the moment. It's just so fascinating now.

# Chapter 3

Today is Wednesday, 27th October, the day that Stephen Turoff said he would be back at his clinic. Steve suggested that I try and ring really early. If he had been away he was sure to be in great demand. Mr Turoff's web site had informed us that there is a seven week waiting list so it was important to fix an appointment. I first tried at 8.30am when the line was engaged. I tried ten minutes later and this time used 'ring back' facility. There was no ring-back by 8.55am so I picked up the phone and dialled again. Imagine my surprise when I found myself speaking to the man himself. "Good morning," I said, "I would like to make an appointment with Stephen Turoff please." "That's me," came the reply and he asked my name. "Hold on please." I heard him leafing through his diary. "Would Thursday, 11th November at 12.30 suit you Shirley?" "Yes thank you," I said. It was as simple as that.

Steve later telephoned his clinic for directions to the clinic. He was told that the fee for the psychic surgery was £25 and that Mr Turoff did not mind friends in the consulting room with videos, cameras etc. He obviously has nothing to hide and he's hardly making much money at £25 a time is he? Why, you could pay more for an aromatherapy massage. Believe me, when you've been told you are incurably ill you are prepared to spend considerably more than this.

Later today I was to pay a visit to one of our church members who lives in Bromsgrove and is also ill with cancer. Eileen is missed very much at church with her cheerful disposition and unstinting help. I called into ASDA to shop and there I met Susan Sprigg. We chatted regarding Eileen and I felt that I must go today and see her. Susan knew that she lived on a housing estate at the top of Hill Lane opposite The Black Cross Inn, but she didn't know what number. I bought flowers in the High Street and set off to find her. I would simply knock a few doors and ask where Eileen Maguire lived. On reaching the top of Hill Lane I gazed around. There were houses to the left and right and on both sides of the road in front of me. I turned left, mounted some steps and knocked on a door. Guess what? Eileen's daughter answered - Spirit had obviously guided me straight there. We chatted at length and I told them my story. Before leaving I left my phone number inviting them to ring if I could help them in any way.

Today, 28th October, Steve and I took a trip to Leicester for our appointment with Ayurvedic doctor Kanu Patel. He asked many questions regarding both my general health and current illness and then disappeared for quite a long time to test a urine sample which I had brought with me. On his return he prescribed several pure herbal remedies, including digestive enzymes and herbs to ensure optimum health for the lungs, and now at last I have my hands on the elusive Carctol. Dr Patel takes the holistic approach to his patients. He feels that where as Western medicine can achieve much with its modern technology, it fails to see the patient as a whole. He feels it is when there is something wrong in the functioning of the whole system that disease is caused. Body, mind and soul have to be looked after. I must take Carctol as part of an Ayurvedic diet; no cow's milk or red meat, no cakes, biscuits, jam or chocolate. Plenty of fresh fruit, green vegetables, seeds and pulses, chicken and fish together with at least eight tumblers of warm boiled water and three sessions of deep yogic breathing! Dr Patel reckons on having to take Carctol for at least two months in order to assess if it is working.

After being on my new medicine for three days I felt well and was coping with the new diet. Also I felt frequent little 'pullings' in the liver area. These are a bit worrying for I really don't know whether it is the Carctol or the cancer that is busy here. The tuggings did cease after a day or so and have not returned so far. On Monday, 1st November I had a second healing session with Jan Higgins, this time we re-located to Val Snow's house. There was much laughter, as before. This must be the particular energy she uses. Her way of describing it, tonight, was that she was being guided to insert energy at certain points of my body and then pull it out through another. She told me that Mom, Auntie Annie and Auntie Flo were again there in spirit and were, this time, waving at me. She mentioned, like Jan Grainger, that I was in a protective spirit bubble so I told her of Jan Grainger's vision and that Olwyn had already started the book's cover before I asked her.

I decided to attempt a chapter on the science of spiritualism which may prove to be a tricky one! There are two books I need to help with research. One is a church library book 'On the edge of the Etheric,' by Sir Arthur Findlay (a must for anyone with a genuine in depth interest in spiritualism) and a book belonging to Alan Perry at church entitled 'From Séance to Science.' I went for a swim during the morning and then returned via church where I thought I may at least be able to find 'On the Edge of the Etheric.' As I parked, I noticed Glenda and Chris's cars and realised it must be 'church cleaning day'. It was great to chat with the girls and up-date them on this 'saga'. We nattered on for about an hour and then I glanced at the library shelves and remembered why I had come. Delcie, our church librarian was sitting chatting too and at this point took out two books from her bag. One was 'On the Edge of the Etheric,' by Arthur Findlay, which had just been returned, and the other she passed over the table to Glenda (Alan's partner). It was 'From Séance to Science' by George W Meek, the other book I needed and not even a library book. She was simply returning it as the girl who had taken out Arthur Findlay's book had borrowed it from Alan. I never even had to get up out of my seat to find my books. This spirit library service is ace isn't it?

The evening of 3rd November, however, did not go so well. I found another breast lump located exactly where the original one had been. The following day all I did was fret. This new little lump is worrying me very much. With all this spiritual activity I was beginning to feel nicely protected in my 'Spirit Bubble' and even quietly confident that this illness had been sent for a reason. But today I am questioning; if spirit is using me then may be they are going a little over the top here, it's getting rather frightening now. The cancer cells are evidently still busy. Now I feel that I am 'out on a limb,' as though I have climbed a high tree and struggled onto the end of a wobbly branch. At present I feel I can either shuffle myself back to the safety of the tree trunk or maybe the meagre branch on which I sit is going to crack and I am going to plummet downwards. It's exactly a week now until I see Stephen Turoff. I really feel I must go but am trying not to pin too many hopes on the visit. From the research I have carried out I really believe in the man but I am well aware that if it is my time to go then nothing will change the outcome. I shall not display my new lump when I see the Oncologist today, nothing must threaten my trip to Turoff, he has to be the next step on my journey. Mel is to accompany us and will video my spirit operation and Jan Tansley, one of our church healing team who not only heals but sees spirit too. I feel she will be able to give us the spiritual perspective on the event.

There is one question which occupies my mind now. If it is my time to pass over, why are the spirit realms wasting so much energy on me and involving so many other people? Something good has got to emerge from all this.

# Chapter 4

I have always had a penchant for having little spiritual chats with people when I feel the occasion demands it. I am one of those 'planters of seeds' and always have been. But now I find opportunities are presenting themselves thick and fast, partly owing to my present situation. I took my daily stroll by the reservoir at the back of my house today and ended up having a lengthy spiritual discussion with a neighbour about passing to spirit. After the discussion he admitted to being really scared of this unavoidable event and he thanked me, telling me I had given him 'food for thought.' Likewise, an old school friend from many years ago phoned as she had heard I was ill. We too discussed spiritualism at length and afterwards she said I had left her feeling inspired. She said she'd felt really down and discussed losing a close friend and the fact that her Mother had been diagnosed with cancer. I felt I had given her a lift and helped her along her pathway a little.

Today is Monday 8th November and my last healing session with Jan Higgins before seeing Stephen Turoff. I feel that the condition of my breast has worsened but that the liver area has improved but I said nothing to Jan prior to healing. We had another really powerful, not to mention, heated healing session. Afterwards, I asked how she perceived my condition. She explained that when passing her hands over a patient trouble spots are felt as 'cold spots'. She said she felt the cold spots on my liver (two on the upper lobe and one on the lower she says), were smaller this week than last, but felt like me that the breast area was altogether colder this week. She feels, like me, that a mastectomy will be needed. We shall see.

It's now Wednesday 10th, the eve of my visit to Stephen Turoff. Susan Sprigg and I have just chatted and she feels the fact tomorrow is Remembrance Day will be significant, especially as I have been given the colour 'red' throughout for energy and healing. She wished me well. I will admit that butterflies are dancing in my stomach as I write. Oh well, off to bed now, I wonder if I'll manage much sleep?

Not a lot is the answer to my last question and I was wide awake by 5.30am. Mel and Jan arrived promptly at 7.15 and the four of us set off for Chelmsford in Essex arriving at the Miami Hotel a good hour and a half before my appointment time. The others disappeared in search of a cafe but I opted for a little snooze in the car, a chance to collect my thoughts. By 12.10 there was no sign of the others so I made my way from the carpark to the small Danbury Healing Clinic situated at the rear of the Miami Hotel. I'm really glad that I went in early and had time to absorb the absolutely incredible atmosphere within. Having paid my £25 I was ushered through to the waiting room. Leaving my shoes at the door as I noticed everyone else had done, I walked into the spiritual shrine which is Stephen Turoff's waiting room. All sorts of people sat waiting, a couple of them obviously in a state of meditation. The walls were literally covered with spiritual photographs, many depicting Stephen Turoff healing with beautiful beams of light entering patient's bodies during healing. Apparently, Stephen Turoff had prayed for God to show his light at the clinic and from the next day 'the Finger of God' photographic phenomena began. There was one amazing photograph taken in the sky above the clinic which revealed a 'tower of white light'. A large portrait of Si Barber, the spiritual healer and Guru, was framed by an orange curtain. Incense burned and beautiful Indian music played. Far from being impatient I could have sat there all day. Steve, Mel and Jan arrived and were soon soaking up the atmosphere with me. At one point Stephen Turoff entered the room, a very tall man resplendent in shocking pink trousers and white T Shirt. He chatted about the weather in his distinctly cockney accent, "Aren't we lucky people to be enjoying this lovely sunshine in November?" I liked him straight away and felt at ease.

Just before 1.00pm my name was called and all four of us squeezed into one of Stephen's small consulting rooms. A healing table took centre place with chairs for patient's friends around the edge. The walls were again a mass of colourful spiritual photography and drawings. By the bedside was a small table displaying Mr Turoff's surgical instruments; a kidney-shaped bowl, scalpel, rods and scissors. There, too, was a small bowl of Si Barber ash. I had previously noticed that patients emerging from the consulting room each had a smear of this ash on their foreheads.

We chatted excitedly for a couple of minutes before Stephen Turoff entered in a brisk and lively manner saying "Come on then, who's supposed to be on this bed?" I leapt up onto the healing table and explained to him, in the briefest of terms, my trouble. He pulled up my jumper and then picked up some surgical implements. I felt a sharp sensation on the right hand side of my abdomen, I heard clacking of a pair of scissors and then his hands kneaded my flesh. It felt like a 'pummelling' and from time to time he appeared to remove something from me which landed with a 'splat' in a bin by the bed. Afterwards, he held his hands over my abdomen for some time. His hands then moved up to the breast area and again he used an implement and there was a sharp sensation. Again scissors were used and matter appeared to be taken from me. Steve was perched on the windowsill above the bed and he said it was difficult to see exactly what was happening but it did appear to him that Mr Turoff's hands were partly disappearing inside me. Before finishing he poured water in my mouth and over my body then dabbed me with a towel. The smear of ash on my forehead and breast area came last. Mr Turoff made no comment or promises throughout the procedure. He simply told me that I must rest for 24 hours, that he had removed a lot of negative energy from me and that he would like to see me again in five weeks time. On rising from the bed I can only say that there was no discomfort whatsoever, but that I did feel rather energised and spaced out. The most notable sensation was a nice warm flow of energy down the right hand side of my body. Before vacating the room I peered into the bedside bin, all that it contained was wet cotton wool.

It is hard to gauge exactly what has happened to you because there is a total absence of blood and inner body tissue. However, we bought the book about Stephen Turoff before we left and in here it is explained that blood and body tissue was causing Stephen Turoff a bad press because of aids risk etc. His surgical spirit team had put their heads together and decided that all blood and body tissue was to be de-materialised so as to be invisible to the human eye.

Once outside the clinic we compared notes about the experience. Jan Tansley is a spiritual healer who sees spirit energy really well and has done since childhood. Her first comment was that to my left, in the corner of the healing room, she had seen a small Chinese type figure with a pointed beard. As soon as Stephen Turoff started to work on me she saw a deep pink energy around my troubled right hand side. Our conversation continued in the car and Mel, who had videoed the whole procedure, turned her video camera on again to film the small scar on my abdomen; it comprised a small circular mark and 2" line pointing towards my navel.

We arrived home at around 6pm and eagerly watched our video. The pink energy was still clearly visible around my right shoulder when we stood outside the clinic. All four of us did notice, at this stage, a lot of energy moving on the patch of wall behind my head. The bottom half of a face was visible to us. I was absolutely shattered and after a hot bath and another photo shoot of my spiritual scar, I was tucked up in bed by 8.30 and eagerly read 'Stephen Turoff, Psychic Surgeon' by Grant Solomon.

Now, as I told you before, Mel had had successful psychic knee surgery by Stephen Turoff fourteen years prior. Her main concern was that Stephen had appeared very different to her back then. She had also felt that he was very overshadowed by spirit when he saw her, even to the point of being in trance state. My new book soon explained this puzzle, it states that spirit has had to 'advance it's technique' so much that light trance control of spirit is now sufficient. This had been done partly to cope with the sheer volume of patients that Stephen now treated and it explains why Mel saw him so differently.

Well it was all a very positive experience and I am looking forward to my next visit. As to how it works, as it has done for hundreds of his patients, it seems to be a matter of the different vibrations of existence coming together, just as clairvoyance is. Physical matter is somehow de-materialised onto a quicker vibration. If it works there has to be scientific explanation doesn't there?
Watch.......this........space.

# Chapter 5

Friends are constantly telephoning me for an update on this 'saga' and I wouldn't have it any other way, although I do take the phone off the hook for an hour or so each afternoon when I go upstairs for my 'ziz'. I have to keep reminding myself that I am supposed to be really ill and should take care of myself. Life is so busy, not to mention interesting, that at the moment I wouldn't swap places with anybody and that's the honest truth.

My good friend Sheila Preston came from Tenbury Wells to see me today. She is a cancer survivor and a strong spiritualist so we found loads to discuss. She and her husband Dave have been seeing spirit orbs in their bungalow lately and she wonders if it could all be a part of the current web being spun around me.

I am well into the book about Stephen Turoff by Grant Solomon now and it is really fascinating. Reference is made to the medium Sue Brotherton and how she was cured of an internal complaint and she speaks highly of him. Now Sue Brotherton was my tutor for a week down at our spiritualist Headquarters at Stansted Hall and I know that she expects the highest and the best from herself and others. Praise by her is praise indeed. Sue now lives in Spain and Mel is either going to e-mail or ring her to have a chat. I had a great surprise this morning when my friend Betty phoned me from Florida to see how the visit to Stephen Turoff went. She has been recounting the story to her friends over there and they too wanted to know the outcome. Seems like these spiritual happenings may be going global.

I have just reached a part of the book that has answered a question for me. It is regarding the 'tunnel of light' which I have mentioned before and which many experience in near death encounters. Dr Khan *(Stephen Turoff's Spirit Guide – see introduction)* concluded a question and answer session for Psychic News through his medium Stephen Turoff. The question was what happens at the deathbed? Dr Khan explained that the etheric body inside us (which is the blue print for our earthly life) has to separate from our physical body before we pass. This body is attached down by our feet by a cord of light. This separation is 'an easing out of the etheric atoms' which have to pass out of the psychic body through this cord of light. The last part of your etheric to pass down this cord to it's new life is your consciousness, so it appears that you are going down a tunnel and the light at the end of it are the etheric eyes which have already transferred. Amazing isn't it? It happens in a scientific way and, I think you'll agree makes perfect sense!

It is now Saturday, 13th November 2004. What a state of excitement my friends and I were to be in by the close of day. Susan Sprigg had said that she would pop in during the course of the day, as she was eager to view the Stephen Turoff video. She even arrived with husband Gary at about 8pm explaining that they had rushed home expecting to baby-sit for daughter Joanne, who it turned out no longer needed her. Anyway, Sue, Gary and I watched the video of spiritual operation twice, paying our attention to what Stephen was doing. I then suggested that we should watch it through once more, this time focusing our attention on the patch of wall behind my head where there certainly appeared to be a lot of energy moving around. We watched this busy patch of energy shifting on what had, after all, only been a plain patch of wall, then Gary suggested that we use the freeze frame facility on the video remote. As I clicked on freeze frame and the film stopped we were to have the surprise of our lives. We began to see, all three of us, the most wonderful little spirit faces, some small, some partially superimposed on each other and other quite large faces. As we watched the energy moved before our eyes and changed the images we saw. Each click to a new frame brought a new revelation, yet more faces, men, women, babies and all of them seemed to be looking towards Stephen Turoff and I, their heads often tilted apparently watching what was taking place on the healing table. Our excitement mounted, Gary pointed out a really large African looking head with a broad nose and then Susan (squeaking with delight by now) pointed out a beautiful little figure of a nun's head and shoulders complete with wimple and collar, she had a lovely face.

By this time near hysteria is breaking out in my lounge (the neighbours must have reckoned there was an orgy at the very least). Fearing that we were experiencing some kind of 'mass hallucination', I rang my friend Gill who lives opposite and told her to come over. Gill is not a spiritualist and I felt it would be wise to have her opinion. She arrived and was soon squealing with excitement like the rest of us. Yes, Gill could see them as well. I phoned Mel and she was soon revelling in the little spirit scenes too. On some frames there were six or seven faces.

Two hours had passed by now and we were still at it. THIS WAS INCREDIBLE. At 10.00pm Paul came in, now this would be interesting, would he see them too? Yes, he could, sitting down on the settee he was soon pointing out yet more faces to us and it was Paul who first noticed the small man's face complete with tin helmet and moustache. I then spotted two other men with helmets. Paul then made a discovery on the left side of the screen and shouted, "look it's a pilot." Everyone surged to where Paul was sitting to view this from the same angle. He was right, a man's face, complete with flying helmet, goggles and ear flaps. About to blow a fuse by now, I shrieked "Of course, think what day it was, the 11th November - Remembrance Day." The figures we were now seeing were soldiers and a pilot to boot! As I mentioned earlier, Susan Sprigg had reminded me that it would be poppy day, but at this time it only tied in with the red energy colour I had been given. Now it was of prime significance to these strange happenings. Mel then remembered too, how it had been nearly 11.00am when we pulled onto the car park at The Danbury Healing Clinic. The eleventh hour of the eleventh day of the eleventh month!

Susan, Gary and Gill went home, Paul went to bed but Mel said she would stay until Steve came home. If ever he couldn't see them he would think I was 'round the twist'.  However, I needn't have worried Steve saw them as well.  As Mel and I chatted into the early hours, she recalled a conversation with famous Spiritualist Medium, Gordon Higginson many years ago.  He predicted that far into the future we would not need Mediums, as the Spirit World would learn to use modern technology to prove it's presence.  He felt that one day we would be able to see them on our TV screens and that was what we had been doing all evening long!

Wasn't it strange, as well, that Medium, Jan Higgins had planned to add another chapter to this book concerning being able to 'peep through the veil at the spirit world'.  That was undoubtedly what was happening here.

Mel had also recalled on her journey up to my house that evening that many years ago she was on a residential course at Stansted Hall.  During a photograph session with a lady called Morag she had found a Chinese spirit face on her photo plate.  Morag had told her then that Mel was a 'Photo Medium'.  Now it appeared that it could be true!

Boy, oh boy, this is really exciting now.  Where are we going with this?

# Chapter 6

Today is Sunday 14<sup>th</sup> November. Val Snow telephoned during the afternoon. We seem to be very much on the same wavelength at present. She was coming out with thoughts about all this that had already passed through my head, talking of highs and lows, light and dark, the most salient being her description of this life as 'the tip of the iceberg' as far as existence is concerned. If you remember, this exact analogy is in my introduction. Val said she felt she ought to attend church that evening, being literally months since she had been. I arranged to pick her up at 7 pm. Our medium was Jackie Hock and her address was so relevant to the present situation that Val and I kept nudging each other incredulously. After the service a group of us chatted and when I mentioned my visit to Stephen Turoff three other people around the table said that they had been to him for psychic surgery, all with successful outcomes. Two of these people I have never met before. One had knee surgery, another had a twelve minute 'heart operation' and the third had eye surgery. The lady who had her eyes done said that Stephen Turroff pushed her eyes through into her sockets and they seem to disappear during the operation and when Mr Turoff had finished she sat up and couldn't see, very alarmed (as you would imagine). Stephen Turoff told her to be patient: he had not re materialised her eye-balls yet. Sure enough in the ensuing minutes they both returned and she has been fine ever since. I asked her husband who had the heart operation how he felt during the procedure. He said that he was taken out of his body to somewhere pleasant and returned when it was all over. There were only about ten of us around the table that Sunday at Church and four of us had been to see Stephen Turroff.

It was great to see Jan Grainger at church again that evening. She is eager to come and see the 'spirits' on the video and reminded me that in 'The Bubble Vision' there had been a sea of spirit faces all sending their love and support.

It is now Monday, 15<sup>th</sup> November and for some reason I admit to being totally exhausted. Maybe the last four days of spirit excitement has taken it's toll. It is very worrying now when I have 'an off day' because of my state of health – a little voice seems to ask "Could this be the beginning of the end?" However, I went to bed this afternoon and after a good two hour catch up ziz, my batteries were recharged and cheeks pink again.

I have also read more of the Stephen Turoff book this afternoon. He has apparently taken a part in several scientific experiments one of which resulted in Dr Khan appearing on a computer screen. The experiment was jointly conducted by Harry Oldfield (biologist and energy scientist) and Dr Gerber, author of a book entitled 'Vibrational Medicine'. At the conclusion of this chapter we are told Stephen also believes that this will be the future and that those unable to communicate naturally will be able to do so via machines. Echoes here of Gordon Higginson's long term view! This causes a little bell to ding in my head. Maybe Stephen Turoff himself would be interested to learn of the spirit faces on our video. Of course it could be 'old hat' to him down at his 'Danbury Clinic' but Mel agreed that we should tell him. He may even be able to point us in the right direction regarding what to do with our precious video. The more I think about this the more I realise that extreme care is needed with this phenomenon, the media likes to rip things to bits don't they. Stephen Turoff's answer-phone informs me that he is away until 22<sup>nd</sup> November so the matter will have to go on hold for the present.

This evening I have my Monday healing session with Jan Higgins. Mel was joining us this time and bringing her video camera. We are anxious to find out if this phenomenon of spirit on TV was likely to repeat itself. We don't know at this stage if it occurred because of the powerful presence of Stephen Turoff or because Mel is starting to develop as a photographic medium. I suppose it could even be me who is the cause. We have to find out who is the medium here. Val had set up the healing table so that we had a plain cream wall as a background for our video and she draped a deep red curtain over the frosted glass dining room door. The atmosphere was, to say the least, lively for this session. There was much jollity and heat from Spirit, I felt is if I was being 'grilled'. Val helped with the healing from my foot end while Jan got on with the hands on stuff. Jan remarked how different my energy was this time; it was plain to see that Stephen Turoff had given me a real boost. She felt that the liver area was okay now and although the breast area was still cold in parts the overall warmth and energy level was better than last week. I still feel that the right breast will have to go and a new underarm tumour gives sharp little tugs from time to time to remind me of it's presence. Again, referring to the Stephen Turoff's book here Dr Khan, through his medium, Stephen Turoff tells a patient off for not having conventional surgery on tumours saying "You silly woman, why have you not been to the hospital". It is clear to me that my visits to Stephen Turoff must be complimentary to orthodox treatment – this seems, indeed, how the psychic surgeon likes to work.

Our healing session progressed with much heat and hilarity (it's a wonder Mel managed to film at all) but Jan assured us that the change of energy was required for the job in hand. As she videoed Mel was making frequent comments about 'moving energy.' The healing was interspersed with snippets of clairvoyance. Ethel & Flo, my Grandad's sisters, were given and then Grandad joined them with his impish sense of humour telling Jan I 'was just right for the tickling' with my arm raised above my head. Dolly or Doll came with Grandad. This was my Nan, Grandad always called her Doll (short for Dorothy). At about 9pm Jan rounded off the session with some crystal healing. Mel then went home but Jan and I resumed, as usual, with tonight's filming. Thank goodness the spirits were just as visible on the Stephen Turoff video, I have this unreasoning, perhaps irrational, fear that they will just disappear. So far they have been visible to most people who watch apart from three, including Paul's friend, Ashley, who went home thinking we were all 'raving mad' no doubt! We played our video and, yes, there were spirit faces again, not so many as before but four lovely little heads could be perceived on the cushion of the armchair. They appeared to be watching the healing procedure. Mel had reported a lot of energy moving at the top of the red curtain. There were several figures here once 'freeze frame' was employed and one of these caused Jan to let out a squeak of excitement. There was 'Sir', her Arabian spirit guide (the spirit who had come through in trance many weeks ago and talked about my condition). Val and I took some time to perceive 'Sir' but once we had he became really clear to us with a jewel in his head-dress. Seeing these spirit faces is rather like looking at these 'illusion pictures.' where you have to see beyond the dots to see what is behind but once you see it it is really tangible to you. Jan and Val, needless to say, went home in a state of happy excitement.

So now we knew that our phenomenon was not isolated to Stephen Turoff's presence – we could repeat it. Mel was informed of the latest findings next morning. She says she will video our service tomorrow night. Maybe this could herald the start of major changes for us all!

That night I must mention waking to complete darkness and seeing and sensing a figure standing over my bed again. It was defined by the deepest pink of dots and as I woke I seemed to be vibrating at a different rate and had to slow myself down again. I felt that this was healing.

This morning I was to receive a card from my Godmother's daughter Jayne. She has just bought a holiday cottage in Yorkshire and kindly offered Steve, Paul and I the use of it when we feel we need a break. The cottage is in the village of Beverley near York. I must remember to tell Jan.

On Wednesday, 17th November I attended my appointment at the Princess of Wales Hospital. I was disappointed when Mr Purser was not there but Dr Khan *(this is not Stephen Turoff's Spirit Guide but one of Mr. Purser's team!)* was most helpful. I explained the breast was becoming uncomfortable but his view was that a mastectomy would be a large trauma for my body and with my liver in such a state he felt that the discomfort and the risk factors would outweigh the overall benefit to me. I explained that I was trying alternative therapies and that I was receiving spiritual healing on a regular basis and asked if I could please have a liver scan to see how it was progressing. Dr Khan was most obliging and has booked me in for another liver scan on 19th November. The results will be available next Wednesday, the 24th so I booked to see Mr Purser.

I decided to attend church that evening. I had half expected to be whisked into hospital and felt I had been granted a 'stay of execution' as it were. I felt quite lively and knew Mel was planning to video the church service that evening. Sue Townsend-Howes was our medium and her philosophy was of a rather serious and heavy nature. Sue usually paces around the platform and her address is interspersed with smiles and laughter. Not tonight, she stood stock-still and we all felt she had been overshadowed by Spirit who was practically using her as their mouthpiece in a very direct manner. Most of what she gave I found very relevant to my situation. I played the middle hymn (choosing 'The world has felt a quickening breath from Heaven's Eternal Shore' as I feel that is what is happening with our spirit phenomenon) and then sat back on the front row for the mediumship. As I sat my eyes were drawn to a little patch of energy which was building up on the dark blue of the church carpet. Before my eyes it formed a man's face, quite a long slim one with a beard, then two or three more partially formed to his side, making a little group. I eventually managed to attract Sue Sprigg's attention and beckoned her to sit by me. I pointed with my toe to the little faces and as she smiled broadly I knew she could see them too. She then found another patch of energy further to the right and as we watched, this too formed into a face. I signalled to Mel, busy videoing from the rear of the church so she joined us and began filming the faces on the floor. Sue (and her husband Gerald who was the chairperson that evening) were quite bemused by us and I hoped we weren't proving too much of a distraction for them. I received a message from Sue and it was all I could manage to lift my eyes from the carpet whilst I spoke with her. She again confirmed to me all the spirit support around me and said I'd been finding different sized white feathers. I had, on my walk the previous day, already found my first. This was a tiny one then a second, a middle sized one and finally a really large one. I had picked them up in the field and then discarded them again. This, Sue reassured me, was the angels keeping watch over me.

On Thursday morning church committee members Alan, Glenda and Thelma came to see the videos. They saw the faces clearly on the Stephen Turoff video and then that of Jan Higgins' guide, 'Sir' on the curtain, together with the four or five small heads obviously watching Jan's healing. One of which, we noted, had the end of his beard overlapping onto my jumper on the table. We then turned to the video of Wednesday night's Church service. There was only the faintest suspicion of faces on the carpet, but when we reached the 'healing' part of the service we had the best results yet. We initially noticed a lot of energy by Gerald on the wall and as we froze the picture two or three heads became visible. As Mel panned across with the camera the faces on the wall followed her in orbs of light across the church to the next healer who was Jan Tansley. As the orbs came to rest we froze the picture and each one formed into a different face. One of the spirits was bearded and wore a turban. Jan reckoned it was her spirit guide, 'Mustopher', but has yet to come and see it. The orbs moved over to where Sue Sprigg was healing me. Some of them came to rest on the floral church curtains. As the faces formed, the energy completely blotted out the busy pattern of the curtains. What was so amazing was the manner in which the orbs followed Mel's camera and the way they moved elsewhere when the healer had closed down and finished. On Saturday night, 20th November Mel and Sue came up to see the church video. Yes, they were overwhelmed by the orbs too, but we also stopped the film during the service and began to find literally dozens of faces here also. They were even forming on Sue and Gerald's clothes on the platform. After watching our latest 'little gem' Susan gave me healing and Mel again filmed, and you'll never guess we had spirit faces once more, some of them we recognised from the previous videos. As Mel filmed, the T.V. (switched off at the time) came into view and when we froze the picture, little spirit faces even formed on the switched off television screen. Very clever, this, we thought. After Mel and Sue departed I mulled it all over and felt that we should now experiment with different 'textures' for spirit to use.

Tuesday evening, 23rd November. Steve came in from having a pint with friend Arthur and we ended up in 'reflective' mode. He said he was only just beginning to realise what an all powerful support network we have all around us. We know so many different groups of people between us, people from hospitals, hospices, runners, and dancers not to mention R.O.S.P.A., Severn Valley Railway. Why, today, I returned home to find an enormous bouquet in the kitchen sink. Opening the card it was from Annie Haywood, President of West Midlands R.O.S.P.A. committee. I've only met the lady once but my church friend Chris Wagg swims with her every morning and had kept her informed of my condition. Today, the ladies at my gym wanted. to know all my news and Betty rang to tell me that her friends in Florida are interested in the Carctol. The support network is there from the spirit side of life too; after all we've seen it on our TV screen!

I must admit to being very churned up about tomorrow's appointment with Mr Purser. Will the liver situation be better, the same or worse? Will he suggest mastectomy? It's all in the lap of the gods.

Wednesday, 24th November. Sad to relate today's appointment has not gone well. The liver scan shows an increase in tumour size, this cancer seems to be ignoring everything. My friends say it is too early to see if 'Carctol' is working but at the moment I am not looking good. I again refused chemotherapy but Mr Purser has suggested a course of radiotherapy on the breast area to see if we can shrink the tumours. If I want a mastectomy afterwards we will consider it. He is trying to create a balance between keeping me comfortable and not putting me through too much, which I understand. It's been a tough day again and I am disappointed but not just for me. If the psychic surgery or the Carctol had worked it would have been such a good advert and I could have helped so many other people. I must stress here that I do believe that Stephen Turoff can and does heal and often cure and I would urge anyone to go and seek his help as I feel he is a wonderful man. If he can't cure me then I must have had my allotted time here on earth. Mr Purser was interested to hear of the spirit people who are appearing. He feels that transition to Spirit must be, as he put it, "Rather exciting" and "Won't it be wonderful not to be restricted by the limits of time anymore." I am to see him again around Christmas.

# Chapter 7

During the 25th and 26th November 2004, the two days following my latest bad news from Mr. Purser, I admit to feeling absolutely awful. 'Positivity' has been my motto for months now but the knowledge that my liver is getting worse on top of the intermittent breast pains has laid me low. Mr. Purser had put a 'pin in my bubble' and my fortitude has disappeared.

At this point in developments, I must mention that I am reading 'Divine Intervention' by award winning health journalist Hazel Courteney. This book, like previous ones I've mentioned, was just handed to me, this time by my friend Val Snow. She had been visiting Stourport (of all places) and felt the urge to go into the library. Never having been in there before she picked up this book straight away and knew she must take it out. The book is the true story of how Hazel Courteney was very painfully and suddenly opened up by Spirit. The process made her desperately ill for several weeks but as she experienced many 'mind blowing' sensations and feelings, she began to hear the voice of Princess Diana. For three months she received astounding evidence from the spirit realms. Reading the cover synopsis, Val had felt that it wasn't really her 'cup of tea' and that at first glance it struck her as maybe being far fetched but still she brought it home with her. The reason she felt compelled to pass it on to me was the photo in the book of Stephen Turoff healing with a beautiful shaft of spiritual energy beaming down on his patient. As I was soon to be off to his Danbury clinic myself she thought I should take it and show it to Stephen Turoff.

Val's first feeling about 'Divine Intervention' was not born out by us both now having read it ourselves. It is an astonishing account of spiritual awakening and whilst reading it I have found numerous parallels between this lady's experience and my own present situation.

Now whilst I make no claims to be 'hearing voices' this lady was 'used' by the Spirit World and became so ill in the process that she really didn't know if she would live or die at the end of it. Likewise my 'guinea pig' status leaves me wondering if I am supposed to survive all of this or whether this saga is to be my 'swan song'. Hazel was impressed to write a book and feels she was destined to do so. Also her life situation is suited to the task given to her by Spirit. She is a columnist on alternative therapies for the Guardian where her story starts and, like myself, has many friends who are spiritualists and alternative therapists. Also, she visited Stephen Turoff for an operation which she described in her book and later we learn that her friend, medium Sue Brotherton, by contact with spirit world confirms 95% of the information which she received from Princess Diana in spirit. Sue Brotherton was the last tutor I had on a course down at Stansted Hall, the Spiritualist National Union Headquarters in Essex and she has served Bromsgrove Church many times. I now think it might be wise to contact Sue and discuss my situation with her.

Now back to how bad I am feeling at the moment. The little jabbing pains within my breast are reminding me of my condition now and because the tumor under my arm is now growing and pressing on lymph nodes, the breast is not draining properly thus becoming swollen. It feels like an alien now and I would rather be rid of it. The liver area suddenly seems to cause me discomfort, almost like the feeling I get with trapped wind - sharp and bloated. Now, as if all this wasn't enough, I am developing stiffness and pain in my neck and shoulder areas and my mind is busy convincing myself that the cancer is on the attack somewhere else now. This afternoon I went to bed and truly felt like this was 'the beginning of the end'. (Two days were spent in this morose state before my next wake up call.)

Steve reckoned that my mind was causing this sudden decline in physical health. He was chatting to his friend Arthur on the phone and as I passed by I overheard him say that it was hardly surprising I felt so much worse after what I had been told. He wished I had never had the second liver scan, but it was my request after all, I had to ascertain the state of my liver in order to make a well-balanced decision on the breast area. That evening both Mel and Susan tried to console me on the phone, saying that the Carctol hadn't had time to 'kick in' yet and there was another appointment coming up with Stephen Turoff. They still felt that everything was going according to the spirit plan.

On Saturday morning, 27th November, not having had a very restful night, I lingered in bed for a while and continued reading my book 'Divine Intervention'. I had reached a part in the story where Hazel is worried about her cleaning lady, Sheila. During Hazel's period of spiritual illumination she had felt drawn to pulse out a healing energy both from her hands and eyes and one morning had laid hands over Sheila's eyes. Her cleaner suffered from Retinitis Pigmentosa and her condition was deteriorating. After this healing session Sheila's eyes improved dramatically and indeed she felt she had recovered. However, several weeks later Hazel was to accompany Sheila on a visit to see her ophthalmic consultant. After examining her, he pronounced that far from improving the disease had progressed and prognosis was grim. Immediately Sheila felt her eyes worsen and was understandably depressed. Hazel felt she must help Sheila but by this time her healing powers had waned as spirit had withdrawn and had grounded her once more. By coincidence, at a health seminar Hazel attends in the course of her work, she meets an optician called Jacob Liberman and relates the story of Sheila's eyes. Dr Liberman tells her that she gave Sheila 'a license to get well' when she healed her, in other words her mind thought it possible and her body followed suit. When she had then been told that, clinically, her eyes had worsened a pin had been stuck in Sheila's balloon (just like mine). The physical effect was immediate relapse. He termed this process 'lethal diagnosis' and it immediately made me feel that perhaps I had subconsciously over-reacted to my own bad news last week. Dr Liberman continued to talk of cases of mis-diagnosis of cancer conditions where patients had taken to their beds, withdrawn and become really ill. It is all to do with the messages which our brains transmit to our body. The mind is all-powerful and this is often what causes disease in the first place. In 'Divine Intervention' Hazel also researches a new electro-magnetic therapy where a patient's natural healthy body frequency is registered and any problem areas can then be boosted with the correct frequency to achieve healing. This is apparent by swimming with dolphins, they can be therapeutic. After all, as we have discussed in my chapter 'Science of it All', the healthy electro frequency ever in our body is activated by electric fields because of our nature as 'vibrational beings'. All of this information, plus the encouragement of friends made me pull myself up by my apron strings yet again. I STILL HAD TO BE POSITIVE. I started on some yoga and deep breathing, ate plenty again and took myself off for a walk in the rain. There's life in the old girl yet.

Val Snow has just telephoned again and as usual says just the right things to me at the right time. She feels that hospitals are, as she puts it, 'places of desperation' and warned me to put a 'protective bubble' around myself whenever I go. Not only is the experience negative on a personal basis, but all the other people around have negativity in their auras too because of the nature of what goes on in hospitals. Now don't get me wrong, all of the Doctors who cared for me have done their best and are compassionate and caring. No criticism is implied here. Of one of the doctors Hazel Courteney encounters in her book she writes: - 'As we shook hands and I looked into his spiritual blue eyes, I knew instantly that he was an awake soul, that I could speak freely and he would not think I was mad'. Echoes of my situation here yet again. This is just how I feel about Mr. Purser. Spirit has placed him there to help me go forward and his receptiveness and spiritual awareness all along have allowed the story to unfold and, indeed, instigated it in the first place.

So today, Sunday, 28th November, I am glad to report that I feel much better. The stiff neck and shoulder have faded. We now believe it is 'a little bug' doing the rounds as Steve now has it and Paul mentioned that he did too when he returned home from college last week feeling 'under the weather'.

I am back on a positive wavelength and I do know that however all this turns out it is meant to be. As I said to my friend Carol on the phone this morning, I didn't want to swap places with anyone else at the moment.

Steve seems to feel strongly about this mind over matter business and informs me that he would like to write the forward for this book.

Val Snow is always a great tonic to me; she sees the funny side of everything and we seem to be tickled by the same things. Lately I do not waste any opportunity for humour and I have taken to answering our telephone with "Hello, Cofton Hackett taxidermists -penguin stuffing department, can I help you?" Val found herself on the receiving end of this nonsense and then sent a get well card with a small penguin on the envelope with a bubble coming from it's mouth saying "watch out she stuffs penguins, you know". The joke has spread to other unfortunates now and Val tells me that whilst Christmas shopping in a rather exclusive confectioners yesterday she came across, of all things, some little fondant filled chocolate penguins. Then when she returned home she opened one of Doris Stokes' books at the very page when she has a clairvoyant vision of what she first thought to be penguins. I even wrote something in the dust covering a snazzy sports car yesterday - "It's something I've often felt I'd like to do and you can't pop off without indulging yourself in some small way, can you?"

On a more reflective note here, Val commented on how clever spirit are in awakening, taking Steve and Paul and bringing them on this journey with me. They have been party to a variety of strange happenings in the house and can both see the spirit faces on the videos. "Have you thought", Val asked, "about how difficult all of this would have been for you if you were ever doubted by your nearest and dearest?" It had been one of Hazel Courteney's fears in 'Divine Intervention' that nobody would believe her and that's why she was so thankful for medium Sue Brotherton's corroboration of her spiritual evidence. "There are so many witnesses to your story Shirley," Val said, "So no one will be able to doubt it". I have the advantage, too, of the spiritual videos; my evidence is on tape. She's so right, dozens of people are now caught in this spiritual net. She also made me think when she said that no matter what happens I will never be 'ordinary' again - quite a thought this, I must make sure that my head doesn't get too big. Val then told me to take another look at the Jan Higgins' video as there was something of benefit to me that I hadn't noticed yet.

I have written this week to Stephen Turoff to ask if this is a usual phenomenon for him. I know he has an interest in spirit and technology from reading his book. Maybe he could advise on what to do with these precious tapes. We realise it could be a disaster if they got into the wrong hands.

# Chapter 8

If this chapter were to have a title perhaps it would be 'preparing to take off'. Today, 29<sup>th</sup> November, Steve and I have been to the Alexandra Hospital, Redditch and seen the Oncologist, Doctor Irwin, regarding radiotherapy. He examined me again and commented on how quickly the tumors on the liver have grown. He offered the hated word 'chemotherapy' again to which I replied, "No thanks, I'd rather pop off next week". He said he wouldn't bully me about it but I could change my mind, to which I responded "There's no point in only putting off the inevitable". He then said something along the lines of 'you are remarkably stoical about all this'. Anyway, he would arrange my radiotherapy and would also try to book Janet Granger in for her's at the same time so that she can come with us.

We then did a little shopping in Redditch and it was a strange feeling for me, I really don't think I shall go again for a while. The world of bustling materialism is already beginning to feel alien to me. I've lost interest and really didn't want anything apart from slippers (with penguins on Val!) and a pair of new 'jim jams' so that I'll look good as I go! Coming home in the car, Steve and I talked of matters we had not touched on before such as funerals and what to do with all my clutter. He says we must be practical and I've offered to make lists for him. Being practical is Steve's way of coping, this I understand.

Last night was very disturbed with coughing fits and hot flushes. I also noticed several bursts of activity with 'the third eye' which took the form of rotating, clearly defined shapes (in monochrome) and I was able to make out a face at one point. I love it when Spirit does this to me.

This morning Sue Curley gave me some lovely powerful spiritual healing and she feels I am well supported from the spirit side of life. She said that the energy they had surrounded me with would protect me from negativity and promised me a good night's sleep tonight which would be great as I was uncomfortable last night and didn't get much at all. She will come and see me again next week, bless her!

I now find I must alternate between negative and positive perspectives when I write. As you can see life is swinging like a pendulum between optimism and pessimism and until we are beyond the point of no return one way or another, this is how it's got to be. It would be truly miraculous to recover at this stage but as Sue Curley said to me this morning, "These tumors can just stop growing you know, it does occasionally happen". I would so like to be a positive advert for Carctol or psychic surgery and spiritual healing, it would help others. But, if I am being ushered into the departure lounge to leave this plane of existence, there is a great excitement at the thought of it. To soon be living in a wider dimension, feeling well and again seeing my beloved family over there, why it fair gives me butterflies to think of it. Steve thinks it will be great over there too. We know we'll have eternity together, but it will be very hard for Paul and Steve in the meantime. I feel so sorry for them, I've already made Steve promise that he'll attend spiritualist church once in a while, in case I need to contact him. I've had a good chat with my friend Nan Buggins who is 90 and very spiritually aware. We've agreed that whoever goes first will come and fetch the other one. She is upset but understands where I'm coming from.

I have also contacted medium Jean Kelford regarding the layout for my book. As I expected she was extremely helpful and currently busy writing her third book on spirit. We chatted at length and she has made me promise that as and when I pass I will contact her straight away to let her know I've landed. If I do she will report it in her next book! So if I am to pass I have my first two tasks lined up for me already, there's forward planning for you!

Meanwhile, I must lift myself up yet again, there's so much to do. This book is my prime concern and this morning Mel came up and we set the computer up together as she is to type some chapters for me. A most unhelpful suggestion came my way today, that I should employ someone else to write this for me because "it's a very difficult thing to do - write a book" yes that's the challenge of it!!! How could I possibly claim it as my book if someone else had written it is beyond me. It may not be the height of sophistication, this work, but it is written with great purpose and I know that spirit is right behind me. If someone else wrote for me it would cease to be 'my book' and become 'a book about me'. There is a world of difference. This has got to be a personal account.

I am very focused once more now; I have to stay well enough to attend the Banbury séance with Jan Higgins on 8th December. Full materialisation is something I've wanted to witness for literally years. Not only do I have to go but I have to write about it too! I only hope. I'll be sitting in total darkness without moving a muscle for two hours - I'm sure it will be well worth the effort. I am looking forward too; to my next visit to Stephen Turoff, so you can see I have to stay well if I can!

I have just been listening to Radio 4's 'The Choice' with Michael Burke. 'The choice' made was that of a daughter not telling her father that he had been diagnosed with Alzheimer's disease. He was obviously a very active and able character but was not even told of his condition. I know every terminal illness situation is different but I feel that this choice is deserved and the poor man had a right to handle the situation in his own way. There may well have been things he wanted to achieve, maybe he would have written a book whilst still well enough. There may have been apologies to be made, bridges to be mended. Sometimes it is not until we find ourselves in a desperate situation that we are driven past our normal capabilities. I feel it is always better to stare truth right in the face. My Mom always taught me never to chicken out as the one person you can't run away from is yourself and you are the one who will lose by it. I would add here that I haven't always been able to do it (I have in the past let myself down) but I have learned along life's way.

# Chapter 9

1<sup>st</sup> December 2004.

Dear, oh dear, why didn't I remember to say "White Rabbits" this morning – R in the month and all that. The morning started quite well but I was bothered by chest pain on my left breast which had been developing over the past two or three days. After doing some 'scribing' and a little light housework I felt inclined to go for a short walk; it was a lovely sunny morning and I mustn't get too unfit. I walked up past the reservoir and noticed I was a little more 'out of puff' than usual. I took a short rest on the bench overlooking the sheep field (it's funny you know since I've been on this no red meat diet I can look those sheep in the eye for the first time – I vow never to eat one of them ever again). I tried a bit of deep breathing (this is part of Dr Patel's regime for me) but there was a very sharp chest pain. I strolled back but by the time I reached home I was rather breathless and this sharp pain got considerably worse. Now what? – chest infection, pulled muscle, impending heart attack, cancer running riot? I decided that I'd better check on this, after all, a neglected chest infection can easily become pneumonia and I don't need anything else. I phoned my neighbour, Margaret, who is a trained nurse and she felt too that I should be checked over. My GP was contacted but as it was chest pain he felt a trip to A & E was called for. So here I am, scribbling away on a hospital trolley having had an E.C.G, chest X-ray and various blood tests. I am waiting to know if I have to stay in overnight.

By 7pm I have seen an assortment of Doctors and nurses and I seem to be a puzzle to them. The E.C.G is fine and the X-ray looks clear at first glance. Blood pressure is fine and so is my pulse and oxygen level. The only thing left to try is a blood test to detect blood clots; apparently my particular form of 'cellular vascular' cancer can cause clotting. At 8.00pm a Sister comes to collect me and take me for an overnight stay in the Medical Assessment Ward. Despite my protests that I am perfectly able to walk, I am 'trollied' to the M. A. Ward where I find I must share with male patients – 'Oh god, how awful' – I WANT TO GO HOME. Steve sat by me and we collected our thoughts and came to a joint decision. Unless the blood test proved positive tonight I was not going to stay. My prime concern, now, was that two doses of Carctol had been missed. I was absolutely ravenous. I could think of nothing more than a hot meal, a hot bath and straight into my own bed with 'Bruno' (my bear). Steve, too, felt that even if I were healthy now, I would probably have caught an infection by tomorrow as there was so much coughing going on. Steve approached the desk where one of the nurses was searching on the computer for the blood test result. It had not arrived. He told them I wanted to go home and a night in hospital was really the last thing I needed in my state of health. At this point I left my bed to join this discussion about me. I said clearly, "Look I am terminally ill and, as far as I'm concerned, if I drop down dead with a blood clot tonight, it would probably be a blessing so can I go now? I'll sign to take full responsibility for myself." Well, there was absolutely no protest, sign I did, and we set off home. I was so tired and hungry. Bruno and I were soon tucked up in bed. To think all this had started only because I thought I might have a chest infection – all I wanted was to see my GP.

Everyone was extremely kind and I know they were doing their best for me, but I'm steering clear of the NHS now, except for my impending radiotherapy.

Today, 2<sup>nd</sup> December, the chest pain has faded and I feel, like Steve, that it is of a muscular nature. I didn't even ring for the blood test result – resignation is the key word today. If I drop down dead now, it would be better than withering away slowly if I do have to go. 'Whatever will be, will be'. It's no use worrying about things that might never happen. For two days I've had no twinges at all from either the breast or liver area, perhaps this latest pain was sent as a distraction – you never know. In any case, it's nice to know that at present my heart and lungs seem to be bearing up to this test.

This evening we received a call from Jan Higgins. Apparently, the gentleman organising the materialisation mediumship I am hoping to see next Wednesday phoned Jan to check that I am still going to attend. He told her that he is holding a healing clinic with psychic surgeon David Thompson in Banbury on Monday and that they had just had a cancellation. He wondered if I would like to fill the place. Jan felt that I should 'go for it.' I have to take everything that comes my way now. She gave Steve directions and said she would ring back David Thompson to say I would be there by 11.00am on Monday, 6th December.

As I sat on the settee hoping that I had made the right decision and that it wouldn't be too much of a journey for me, I glanced at my dark green lounge carpet to see a patch of energy form itself into three perfect little spirit faces. Two of them I recognised from the videos. Well if I needed a sign this was it. Those little faces, if they were trying to tell me anything it was "Yes, go on, do it".

Jan Higgins also informed me that she came across a magazine article when on a course in Manchester earlier in the week. It was about a new drug being trialled for cellular vascular cancers. She ripped it out, when no one was looking and will let me have it on Monday when I see her for healing.

By bedtime tonight I was feeling really ill. I had lots of little jabbing pains in my joints and felt feverish. Now what was this? I felt less worried when Paul said he felt the same and Steve went up to bed early because he was stiff and aching. Obviously a little 'bug' as though I needed anything else to cope with.

Today is Saturday, 4th December and Steve has organised a Christmas meal for all the friends he walks with during the year. He decided, on retiring early from work at the age of fifty, that before he was sixty he would have walked a marathon in every county of England, Scotland and Wales. It has been a great way of bringing folk together and now there is a 'hard-core' of lads who accompany him on many of the walks. So today, all walkers and spouses are to meet for a festive meal. I've felt really well today, I think the aforementioned 'bug' affected me more than I realised. It is very difficult to gauge my true state of health now, as you will appreciate. We were to meet at 12.00 noon at a local pub and as we went out to the car Paul said "hey, mom look what I've found on my mobile phone" he passed it to me and there were two spirit faces on his mobile phone screen. One was the large African, broad nosed face that we first saw on the Stephen Turoff video and a much smaller face emerging within his larger one. Now I think you'll have to agree that Spirit are being quite clever here.

We were on our way to a very mixed social gathering and I was obviously going to be talking of recent events both spiritual and health wise (I cannot separate the two now). Obviously I couldn't take the video so Spirit had created a small portable version on Paul's mobile which we passed around to everyone's amazement. Even friends Robin and Jan, who I think would term themselves 'Humanists' and feel there is nothing after this life, were quite amazed by my story backed up by the evidence on Paul's mobile.

On Sunday afternoon I invited Val Snow up as we felt an urge to take a fresh look at the healing video with Jan Higgins. I had found a Chinese head which we had missed before and Val thought it might be her guide. However, we searched and searched to no avail, he could not be found this time. One thing Val did point out to me was a rainbow on the curtain which if you remember was draped over the room door. I could clearly see the arc of it but Val was able to see all the colours too. Val was impressed, too, by the spirit orbs on the church healing video and we also saw here the complete figure of an elderly lady, missed until now.

Spirit are certainly getting on with their use of modern technology and they were quite wise too in employing me in their scheme because I just can't keep any of it to myself. As I said before, I am the preverbal 'seed sower' and I reckon there could be a few unexpected germinations after today. I'm really looking forward to the psychic surgeon on Monday and the séance on Wednesday.

# Chapter 10

Today, Monday, 6<sup>th</sup> December, Steve and I travelled down to Banbury to see healer, medium and psychic surgeon David Thompson. He is also the physical medium I am to see on Wednesday evening, obviously a man with many spiritual gifts. We arrived far too early and sat drinking coffee in the car until the sanctuary opened. 'Jenny's Sanctuary' is built in the cottage garden of Roy Gilkes, right out in the Banbury countryside. Jenny is Roy's daughter who passed to spirit at the age of twenty nine. So much communication was received from her that it was decided to build a spiritual sanctuary in her memory for the development of spiritual gift and the comfort of the bereaved, particularly those who have lost children. The place has a very special feel about it and comprises séance room, healing sanctuary, physical room and a large reception area. Having told you of our very early arrival, I found the wait both relaxing and stimulating. Framed on the walls were children's messages and drawings from Spirit, accomplished during strictly controlled séances. Also, an apport hung in a box frame. Apports are gifts from Spirit which they dematerialise from somewhere else on earth and then re-materialise inside the locked séance room. This one was a small toy dog which Spirit said they had taken from a department store and the other, a more recent spirit gift, was a small, fuzzy, mauve material ball. Apparently, Roy Gilkes told us, the little spirit girl responsible was only ten years old and told the séance that she was still learning to do this and could only at present manage 'soft articles'. There to view, also, was a shelf displaying various spiritual writings received through mediums at séances. Several were in a totally foreign script, one having been written in what was identified as an ancient Chinese form of writing. It had been checked by an expert and was found to be word perfect.

We waited until 1.00pm for David Thompson and his assistant. He came and chatted to us, explaining that all eleven of us would be seen whilst he was in continuous trance, as one patient exited the healing sanctuary the next should go in. I was to be third in line. As I awaited my turn, I glanced down at my feet to see, once again, two spirit faces perfectly formed on the carpet. Both I recognised from three evenings ago when Jan had invited me here. One face was, again, the thin, dark, Jesus like face with dark eyes and moustache and beard joined together. The second was, again, the plump, female one with a lot of hair and side parting. I feel now that this lady was my Nan; Jan Higgins recognised her on the healing video but I was unable to spot her. Jan said it would make sense for Nan to be around us. Nan had cancer at thirty-six, both her breasts were removed but lived until she was ninety-two. She would want to help and encourage me.

I entered the healing sanctuary and was directed to a chair opposite David Thompson, now obviously in trance. 'Doctor Stravinski', David Thompson's spirit guide, spoke to me via David in what I would call a Swiss accent. We sat facing each other rather like a conventional consultation and he asked me what my trouble was. I was then told to lie on my back on the healing table. The Doctor's assistant explained that although he would lay his hands on me I was to take care not to touch him at all; as this can be dangerous when a medium is in trance. The Doctor was the perfect gentleman throughout, asking if it would be permissible to touch the breast area through my jumper. When he had finished this hands-on healing, from which I felt a lovely warm surge, he asked me to turn onto my front. The assistant made me comfortable and then Dr Stravinski asked her to undo my bra strap. He then worked on the liver area on my back. A towel was placed over my head during this part of the procedure and I experience a pummelling sensation (as with Stephen Turoff) but this time no physical surgical implements were used at all. I felt a warm trickle down my back, which I would imagine was warm water. Dr Stravinski then made quite painless pinching movements as though he was removing something from me. He then told his assistant he would like to work underneath the right breast and asked her to prepare me. In the same discreet manner I stripped to the waist and the lady covered me in a towel. The same pinching and removing sensation was then employed under my right breast, again with no pain whatsoever. I would think that this was in the area containing the smaller upper liver tumors. On completion Dr Stravinski asked me how long the orthodox medics had told me I had left. I replied, "Six months but that's now two months ago". "This is not to be so," he said, "you will live; there is much for you to do yet". He told me that cancer need not be terminal and that my tumors would very gradually flatten and then de-materialise. He recounted the details of a Chinese lady, supposedly terminally ill with a tumor on her thyroid. He said that he had treated her first as he had treated me and that eventually when her consultant checked her there was no tumor to be found at all. He assured me that this would also happen to me. We discussed the orthodox treatment I had received and I told him about the Carctol. I said that I had been informed from Spirit that I was to be used as a guinea pig and that I was currently writing a book. He said that he wanted to be included in my book and made me promise to send his medium a signed copy. He even spelt his name for me and his assistant wrote it down on a slip of paper. I thanked him for his valuable time and bade him goodbye. Well, what an experience and, unlike Stephen Turoff, here was a promise from spirit that I WILL BE WELL AGAIN. I walked out of the healing room feeling great, my positive energy restored again. When he had finished David Thompson said goodbye to Roy Gilkes and other patients. Altogether it was a great trip, interesting spiritually. We met some lovely folk and once again I feel that I am on track.

Tuesday 7<sup>th</sup> December.

This morning I received an early call from Val Snow. She awoke early this morning and was strongly influenced by Spirit and she thought of me. Val has started to hear Spirit as well as see; she has been told that this would happen. She heard the 'clicking' of jig saw pieces going down into a puzzle and felt that everything was 'coming together' regarding my saga.

The key to my recovery is to hold in place this positive energy without someone filling me up with negativity once again. In order for the work done by Dr Stravinski, yesterday, to do it's job and de-materialise the tumor, I had to stay positive. Others around me had to think of me as being well, not as having cancer. The only way this cancer was to be thought about was as disintegrating. I must at all costs avoid hospital, apart from going for my radiotherapy. Val also said she had been given the symbol of the rainbow again and felt I should focus on its colours. The rainbow is a symbol of promise. Was the promise of me being well again? I then told Val that there was a fan light over the door yesterday at Jenny's sanctuary. Steve too had noticed it and the light shone through it. This of course tied up with Val feeling we had to take a fresh look at the healing video on Sunday. We couldn't find the Chinese man, but it obviously wasn't important, what was vital was finding the rainbow!

Tuesday afternoon, 7th December

I have to admit something here which I know is, maybe, going to seem a little out of context, but I can't help it, I'M ANGRY! I have just returned from a stroll down to my local post office and I'm really glad that earlier on Mel telephoned me just as I was slipping my jacket and shoes on to make the trip. Had I been ten minutes earlier I would have probably been caught up in an attempted armed robbery no less. Luckily someone at the premises adjoining the post office saw the thugs getting out of their car, complete with masks, guns etc. They then fled and apparently robbed a different post office not far away. Now about three years ago the previous tenants of our post office were bound and gagged and held at gunpoint in a robbery. Keith and Liz, not in the best of health, were never the same again. Confidence shaken, they lived in constant fear afterwards and soon decided to retire. Doesn't it just make your blood boil - these nasty people who don't give a damn about anyone else and think it's ok to take what belongs to others instead of working for it themselves.

Not long ago, my son Paul had his moped taken from our driveway and last week two houses in our road have been burgled. I could rant and rave about the acts of vile specimens for a whole chapter. Society, in my opinion, is far too lenient with these low elements. I might not sound very spiritual here but ten years of working in a Magistrates' Court plus seeing the awful effects these toads have had on the lives of so many decent people has made me this way. Last Christmas, a very dear friend of mine was burgled. She had lost her husband earlier in the year and lost countless irreplaceable items of great sentimental value. Her nerves were shattered for some months and she has had to turn her house into a virtual 'Fort Knox' to feel at all safe. How do these vermin sleep at night? The law is far too soft on them and I feel the only way they will pay for their vile conduct is when they pass to spirit. For we are told that we all pass to a state of vibration suited to our spiritual development. Those of the natural low and like vibration end up in the same realm or sphere, it's a case of 'birds of a feather' I suppose. We are told that those who have lived in evil, selfish mode and harmed others will dwell in a dark miserable place of much lower vibration than our earth plane. Indeed, it is as the bible tells us "As we sow then shall we reap". So I hope that the 'toadies' who hurt Keith and Liz and the ones who burgled my friend, Joyce will one day be really miserable in this dark place where they will one day dwell with their own kind! Ugh! We are told, however, that everyone has the opportunity to progress if it is their soul's desire, and it is a matter of their own choice. They will feel the hurt they have caused others and made to atone for their terrible behaviour and can then progress towards the light as our seventh Spiritualists National Union principle states "Eternal Progress open to every Human Soul"

# Chapter 11

Tonight is the psychic séance at Banbury. It is Wednesday, 8th December 2004. I have tried to rest this afternoon but butterflies of anticipation are fluttering inside me. There is nowhere on earth I would rather be going to but I am wrestling with one of my 'gremlins' - that of claustrophobia (I don't do lifts!). The thought of being locked in a totally dark room for two hours is making me somewhat anxious. I have sent out thoughts to Spirit to give me the strength because I know full well that if I 'chicken out' I will always regret it. Steve returned home at 4.00pm and drove me to the school where Jan Higgins teaches and I went with her. We arrived at 'Jenny's Sanctuary' at around 6.30pm.

I would judge there to have been about 35 people present, all of them excitedly chattering in the reception area. I had spotted medium Sue Tomlinson when we parked the car. If you recall, she was the lady who gave me a message right at the beginning of my illness - it was great to see her here. People were preparing for the séance, drinking water or tea and there was a queue for the loo. We were told that absolutely nothing could be taken into the séance room; all watches, jumpers and jackets were to be removed all pockets completely emptied.

At 7.15pm we were all individually invited into the séance room and searched. A lady searched the females and a man the males. Every pocket was inspected and finally we were passed to a gent who scanned us electronically as a final check, it was on a par with Heathrow! Our names had been placed on the seats and apparently we were arranged 'as guided by Spirit'. Jan and I were on the second row but fortunately right up close to the medium's cabinet. I was also situated on the end with a decent space in the corner. There was only one item to my left in the corner and that was a steel bowl full of water on the floor. Apparently, Spirit uses it as part of their chemistry for producing ectoplasm. Everyone was so friendly and we chatted happily amongst ourselves. I do admit to feeling rather apprehensive as the door was closed, bolted and finally sealed around with black tape. There was obviously to be not a chink of light. Our medium, David Thompson, was tied into his tubular steel chair using cable ties, both ankles and wrists being securely fixed to the chair's frame. Cable ties were also fixed through every buttonhole of his cardigan and through the fabric of his cardigan on the opposite side. The poor chap was also gagged and the gag securely tied and fixed with a cable tie. There was clearly no way that he would be able to move at all. Paul, the circle leader, gave us final instructions. We were to sing and link hands as directed. We should comment if Spirit touched us in any way as this was to be a 'shared experience' and we all needed to know what was taking place in the pitch dark. We were not to fidget or blow our nose and you had to be taken seriously ill to be able to exit. Fortunately, no such problems arose and our leader, Paul, only had to calm us on a couple of occasions, sometimes due to hilarity and sometimes due to the recipient of a spirit message being overcome by emotion. We were told at the outset that we must try to hold back emotion as it adversely affects the conditions that Spirit are striving to create. By 7.30pm preparations were complete. A young man called Alex was to operate the CD player and Paul, our circle leader, was to have his hands held on either side to ensure that he did not move from his seat. He assured us that should he need to move from his seat for any reason he would tell us that he had vacated his chair. The light bulb from the fitting by the door was now taken out and for a while we sat in the dim glow of the medium's red light. This was gradually dimmed and then turned off and we were in utter darkness. Nora, a tiny lady '94 years young', opened beautifully in prayer for us and then we burst into our first rendition of 'Jerusalem', everyone singing their heart out to raise the vibrations. Before long, our circle leader announced that he had just been tapped on the shoulder and we had begun.

The first spirit voice literally boomed out from high up in the centre of the circle. His name, he told us, was Sir William Crawford. He spoke in a powerful, authoritative and educated voice. It was fascinating, this voice, so clear and strong and seemingly 'coming out of nowhere'. So this was direct voice; the Spirit World fashioning an ectoplasmic voice box by various scientific and chemical means so that the spirit forms can press their face into it and, as they use their own etheric voice, our earthly atmosphere is vibrated and thus becomes audible to us. Sir William welcomed us, spoke briefly and then announced that he would take any questions we might have. Jan Higgins got in promptly with a question concerning the promised de-materialisation of my tumours. How was this possible she enquired and even cheekily suggested a 'demo,' presumably on me, there and then! Sir William's reply was clear and precise. The spirit doctor, by altering the vibration or electrical field of the entranced medium or psychic surgeon, can then pass spiritual energy through the physical body because of it's vastly faster vibration and literally breaks up or 'dematerialises' the growth. 'Dematerialise' simply means transferring body tissue to a fast spirit vibration so that our own physical laws no longer apply.

Sir William said that if Dr Stravinski had claimed this was done then it was done. A practical demo was not feasible, he stated, and I think I might have been somewhat relieved here, but you know me, I would probably have 'gone with the flow'! He said also that such psychic surgery could be achieved in the blink of an eye without the patient being aware at all. Dr Stravinski, however, said that it would be a gradual process. We will have to wait and see and I am still very much aware that if my earthly span is finished then it is my time to go. Jan then further questioned whether it was always necessary for physical surgical implements to be employed in psychic surgery. Sir William's reply was that it was now becoming less necessary as Spirit had now learned to direct their energy as a laser; indeed he drew a parallel here to how orthodox surgery on earth now often uses lasers in order to avoid tissue damage. Both Jan and I thanked him for his explanations.

It was as Sir William took his leave of us that we heard the most amazing sound of the ectoplasmic mask being drawn away. It was loud slurping suction which I can only describe as being an organic sound, really strange. We were to hear it as each spirit entity took it's leave of us. Some of the sounds were louder than others but always this strange suction. I noticed that visiting spirits who were not practised at using their masks took a while to find the correct technique. The laboured breath as they tried to synchronize their etheric speaking with the ectoplasm of the mask was clear - very eerie. Not surprisingly, those well schooled in this manner of communication, (like Sir William Crawford) spoke clearly and directly from the very start. I found their 'mask' sounds the most stunning element of the séance and definitely not for the faint hearted!

I managed to control my claustrophobia quite well and despite the fact that there were some fairly dramatic temperature changes, dependant on spiritual activity, it was not as hot as I expected. When Sir William had taken his exit, we were joined by Timothy, a young lively cockney spirit who chatted loud and long. The spirit trumpet made a rapid take off and could be seen darting energetically across the ceiling then back down to our level. The luminous paints around both ends of it making it clearly visible to us. Tim explained that, at that moment, ectoplasmic rods were being used to manoeuvre the trumpet. He then explained that he was taking over the process and many folk on the front row were then tapped vigorously on the head - shouting out when they had, to let us all know. I have never felt such a desire to be hit on the head by anything in my entire life, but it wasn't to be. When you are on a search all tangible proof is so important to you. Tim informed us that he was to try and show himself to us and asked circle leader Paul for a small amount of red light. We all sang our hearts out but on this occasion it wasn't to be despite lengthy and painstaking effort. Having given up on full materialisation he said that he would walk round the interior of the circle and show us his hand by using a tile which had been placed in the centre of the circle. This tile was made luminous by Spirit and as Tim walked around I could clearly see his four fingers and thumb glowing through.  At the same time he gave way to his exuberance by clouting us on the head again with the trumpet.  His next little job was removing some beads from one lady and a scarf from another.  When he announced that he had removed these, two ladies in the circle verified that they were missing.  From this point, Spirit informed us that they would take over the operation of the CD player and then confused us dreadfully with the singing, much to everyone's amusement.  Jan said that this spirit control of the music was a new development.

The most emotional part of the séance was the communication with loved ones.  Five spirits came through including two small children. The first communicant gave his name as Ray and Tim said that he belonged to Nora, the elderly lady who had opened in prayer for us. Ray took a while to adapt to the ectoplasmic voice box but managed to send his love and managed to mention two other family names which were accepted.  He also made us laugh by saying that he had seen Nora on a bike recently.  She said, "Yes, but it was a recently acquired exercise bike and that it proved that Ray had indeed been in her home of late".  He also said that she had lost her footing on it recently.  Yes, she had.

The most moving and evidential message came through to a lady who was on a visit from Australia.  Tim shouted again from the vicinity of the cabinet that further spirit communicators were waiting.

The first two communicators had considerable difficulties in making themselves heard at first and emotion was obviously running high. Paul kept asking the lady recipient to hold back her emotion - it was so palpable to us all.  The spirit then said quite clearly "Thank you for keeping your promise" and his parting message was "I've just got the lad with me".  Tim then shouted from the box that he had Bill for the lady also. She said that he was her father and the voice then came to her with "Leoni, Leoni".  Leoni then thanked her father for coming to her on the night he had died.

Following the séance, I swapped phone numbers with Leoni. I wanted to ascertain why her message was so evidential so that I could include it here. There was an emotional farewell here as they parted, again to an incredible 'slurping' noise when the mask was drawn away. I will hopefully be able to add this lady's perspective to the book when I have spoken to her.

The last contacts were those of two small spirit children. Tim asked, "Where's Lisa"? The lady immediately in front of me responded, "You lost a baby, Lisa"? "Yes," she said. "Was it twins"? "I don't know," she replied. "well," he said, "there were twins, a boy and a girl and they've come to visit you". Then the sound of a small child's feet was heard running across the carpet from the direction of the cabinet. The small footsteps stopped in front of Lisa and I could clearly hear the breath of this little child through the mask. Lisa, struggling to hold back her tears said to the spirit, "Oh, I can feel your tiny hand in mine", the other hand she said was resting on her knee. Then, I heard this tiny voice say; "Love you mummy". The first child then, very audibly, ran back to the cabinet and the second child ran over to Lisa. Again I heard the breathing and again the word 'mummy'. When both children had finished speaking the ectoplasmic mask was heard to de-materialise.

After these five spirit visitors, two more big surprises were in store. An American gentleman, Dr Slate, arrived and went directly to a couple in the circle who, he said, had seen his bag. The gentleman in circle then confirmed that he had indeed purchased the bag off this once famous American physical medium. Dr Slate then requested that we sing as he needed the vibrations raising in order to carry out some experiments. Dr Slate told us that had used this bag to keep his slates in which spirit chose to write on, also phenomena of all sorts would emerge from inside it. Tim then informed us that Dr Slate was going to do something with the wooden rings which were shown to us centre-circle at the beginning of the séance. Dr Slate then spoke to a lady at the front of the circle and enquired of her; "These your beads lady"? "Yes," she responded. "Well, you have them back", he insisted. "I have no place for them". Dr Slate then bade us farewell and the music "What a Wonderful World" was played and we sang most heartily to it. As it neared an end, a powerful voice was added to it, that of the great man himself, Louis Armstrong. He introduced himself with great exuberance and shook hands with several people on the front row. His footsteps were very heavy and noisy and several sitters commented on how large and warm his hands were. He then announced his intention to play the harmonica and did so beautifully using the harmonica which was seen centre circle before the séance started. Jan had told me that Louis was a frequent visitor to the circle. My, this was certainly going to take some proving to those not in attendance.

Tim told us that as the energy was waning we must close the circle. Everyone stayed seated as instructed whilst medium David Thompson's special coming round song was played. It was a further five minutes or so before the light was finally turned up. Paul asked for the light by the door to be turned on as for some reason the red light was inoperable. The medium was far from back with us and we maintained silence as he came round. We were all there to witness the removal of the cable ties, still all in tact and needing to be cut apart with pliers. However, his cardigan was now clearly on back-to-front and two wooden hoops (about 7" in diameter) were now in place on his two forearms. As both David's ankles and wrists were still in place, tied to the steel chair frame, this must have been a demonstration of dematerialisation; there was just no other way to get them on.

The following morning I received the promised phone call from Leoni, the Australian lady at the séance. As she spoke with me, it became apparent what an incredible emotional message she had received. The first gentleman who came through had been her father-in-law, Jess, who she had never met on this earth because he had been shot down whilst flying a Lancaster bomber during the Second World War. Her husband was just four and a half months old at the time. Sadly, this lady had lost her husband with cancer earlier this year and her last promise to him had been to visit her father-in-law's grave in Belgium. So now it's possible to see how incredible the words: "Thank you for Belgium" were and also the significance of this spirit's parting words: "I've got the lad with me" i.e. his own lad, Leoni's husband. I asked the lady if her father-in-law had touched her. "Oh my, yes", she said. Apparently, as she had cried, he had held her face in his hands which were warm, and he moved his thumb across her cheeks to wipe her tears - Wow! I asked her if the second voice was clearly indentifiable to her as her father. "Oh yes," she said. He called her by her name which, she said, she had not revealed to anybody in the circle. We chatted for some time and she made me promise to let her relative over here know when my book was published.

# Chapter 12

Today, the day after the séance, I have to inform you that, health wise, I am feeling absolutely diabolical. I feel breathlessly tired and have an acute pain in the region of my solar plexus. By afternoon I was feeling in need of some form of medical help but Steve, loathed to call any medics in, suggested I get some spiritual healing. I rang Jan Tansley and, hearing the distress in my voice, she set out immediately and arrived within twenty minutes. As she entered the lounge she first commented on the vast amount of spiritual energy in the room, and then as she began work on my aura she said that a terrific amount of energy was pumping out of my solar plexus. It appears I had been quite dramatically opened up spiritually and the Chakra in question needed 'calming' and even closing down for a few minutes. *(Note: The Chakras are the spiritual energy centres in the human body and are linked with our physical health. The word comes from the Sanskrit language and means 'wheel'. There are seven major Chakras that form the etheric spine: Base, Sacral, Solar Plexus, Heart, Throat, Brow and Crown. Our existence 'revolves' round these.)* This she did and started to return to normality (I'm not too sure what 'normal' is these days really). I recounted the events of the séance the previous evening and we both felt that it had drained my energies. The ectoplasm for all that spirit actually would have been drawn from sitters as well as the medium. I had been in a state of high excitement all day and the journey there was quite taxing. I also had to psyche myself up to coping with my claustrophobia, it was no wonder I felt so ill.

Susan Sprigg re-enforced Jan's diagnosis and advised me to have a little word with Spirit explaining that whilst I was happy to work for them, would they please keep away for a few days as I was physically drained and needed to compensate. Healers however were very welcome to draw close.

On Saturday evening, 11<sup>th</sup> December, we had tickets to see the music group St Agnes Fountain at Holy Trinity Church, Lickey about a mile away. My Godmother, Audrey and friend Nan Buggins were to accompany us. I really felt it an effort to go out and I did have an awful pallor about me. By the interval I was very uncomfortable and Steve brought me home. I took a hot bath but started to experience a sharp pain on my right hand (liver) side. The pain I had endured for the last two days was on my left hand side and this had now disappeared, just like the pain of the previous week, which had been left undiagnosed. My body is certainly full of surprises - it's most disconcerting. I do not know if the pain is the cancer, the Carctol taking effect or the de-materialisation as promised by David Thompson. It's all an enigma. Anyway, by 1.00am I was in considerable pain and Steve called out an emergency doctor who arrived at about 3.00am. He prescribed a stronger painkiller. On Monday we are going to consult Dr Jemell re pain relief etc. It is looking extremely likely now that it's my time to 'move on'.

Val Snow, as usual, phoned when I was at a particular 'low ebb' and knew exactly how to cheer me up and set me back on course. I had to be completely self-indulgent and listen to my body. "The body wants to heal", she said, "It's natural". "The cream will always rise to the top." I was to see my tumors as strawberry jelly gradually dissolving whilst awaiting my stronger pain relief.

Paul sat on my bed chatting and trying to divert my attention. He zoomed in with his mobile phone taking a shot of my bear 'Bruno' and I. There on his mobile screen was a spirit face on my pillow. We then spent a good ¼ hour taking mobile photos of my bedroom, the stairs and landing. There were loads of perfect little spirit forms. Ladies and men and one little spirit body even moved around for us. They really are everywhere - there's just no denying it!

On Sunday (12<sup>th</sup>) I battled on, now the stronger pain relief was taking effect. However, I was extremely dopey and sleepy and it was an effort to stay awake.  By the evening I felt a little nauseous but ate my evening meal as usual.  This turned out to be a big mistake as I lost it all within ½ hour 'On the big telephone to God' so to speak.  Steve felt it could be the Kapake tablets and this was confirmed by Dr Wijnberg, my G.P., the following morning when he called to see me. He has suggested that I alternate between the Codeine based Kapake pill and Paracetamol to find the level which suits my system.  I now have some 'stand by' pills for sickness and he suggests that Macmillan nurses should be contacted at this stage of my illness.  I have very mixed emotions on this one as you might well imagine.  However, I know that clinically I am terminally ill and I have to consider my immediate future contingency plans which have to be in place.  I know these already; I've been through the process with Mom and Dad.  As I said to Steve today, it's a pity there isn't a bus with 'Spirit World' on the front.  You could just hop on and wave goodbye to your friends with a smile and a 'see you later,' but sadly, there is usually a lot of suffering before we are allowed to pass.  Perhaps it should be seen as a right of passage.  It's easier for pets, really, isn't it?  We say, "Oh we had Fluff put down, it was the kind thing to do." It certainly seems attractive to me now - a magic 'end it all pill'.

Now, on a more positive note, Jan Higgins and Val Snow arrived this evening to give me healing.  I lay on the lounge settee in almost complete darkness with Val working on my head and shoulders whilst Jan worked on my bad right side.  Tremendous heat was again generated and this time we all kept quiet as Jan was obviously overshadowed or in light trance as she worked.  Val Snow said she appeared to be taking implements from a 'spiritual' bag and then used them on me.  Psychic surgery could be the next step for Jan as she is already a strong trance medium and a powerful healer.  Perhaps this is a positive thing that will come out of my illness, like the appearance of Spirit on video and mobile phone screen.  I must mention here, also, that Steve and I have just picked up some developed photos and we have one taken at Bromsgrove Spiritualist Church.  It shows spirit heads on the steps up to the rostrum.  Jan Tansley said she saw them at the service, with Sue Townsend-Howes, which we videoed.  I had taken a photo as an experiment and again it had paid off. I suspect that, undoubtedly, a lot will be gained in so many ways even if I do pass to Spirit, particularly with the spiritual seeds I have endeavoured to sow along my way. However, what a fantastic story it could be if, even at this eleventh hour, I managed to recover. I would become 'an ad.' for so many alternative treatments and belief systems. It's still very exciting, I must admit.

This morning (December 14<sup>th</sup>) Val has just phoned. After leaving me last night, she and Jan went to Redditch to sit in circle with two friends Meenah and Simon. I will mention here that during circle Val clairvoyantly saw a gentleman with a very long sharp-nose who she did not recognise. After circle, Jan asked if she could go into trance, not a thing she generally does during ordinary circle work. The others agreed and she quickly went into trance with a new spirit coming through. A deep voice announced that he was Dr Joseph Bell from Edinburgh. Val said the voice was struggling to come through. It seemed difficult whereas usually Jan's voices boom through strong and clear. He spoke of Jan's friend who is very ill and said that he was working in conjunction with Dr Pratt and Dr Pringle and that the help being sent to me was of the very highest. He said however, that he could not confirm what the outcome of my case would be.

The following morning, Val looked up these Doctors on the Internet. Dr James H. Pringle was indeed a surgeon and graduated from Edinburgh University. He lived between 1863 and 1941. He was one of the first to base treatment on radiological control. Val was also amazed to find his portrait on the Internet. He was the long nosed gentleman she had seen in meditation before Jan went into trance! An explanation was also to follow as to the difficulty with Dr Bell's voice. Apparently, whilst searching the net, Val found anecdotal information on Dr Bell. Apparently he spoke with a strangulated voice after contracting Diphtheria. He sucked out some diphtheria poison trying to save a child's life; he was commended by Queen Victoria for this.

I am awaiting some notes on this trance information which Meenah is kindly forwarding to me. Today, Thursday, 16<sup>th</sup> December was to have been my second visit to Stephen Turoff but my body and my common sense told me that I should cancel. Six hours in a car when you're ill is not really a good idea, so I cancelled yesterday.

Mel and Susan came to take me out for a quick trip to local garden centres and we had a great time, stopping for lunch. I feel really well today and somewhat surprised. A lady phoned me this morning. I answered with my usual "Hello, Cofton Hackett Taxidermy - penguin stuffing department, can I help you?" only to find that the lady chuckling on the other end was the Macmillan nurse who Dr Wijnberg had put in touch with me. She sounds lovely and will pay me a visit on the 6th January (probably got me down as a nutcase already). I still swing between feeling it's my time to go and then feeling that perhaps Spirit will do their stuff and I'll be well again, but amidst all this is no despair, despondency or 'clinging to straws.' I am content that what will be, will be. My pathway is set and I know things will transpire as they should. I know that those who I love will be there to greet me if I pass to Spirit and I also know how many great folk are here rooting for me, helping me and sending me healing. So what ever happens, I'm so lucky, aren't I? I wouldn't swap places with anyone, anywhere!

# Chapter 13

Over this last week-end (18th and 19th December) my spirit has been low. I have felt extremely tired and am not enjoying food - just making myself eat. It's hard to say whether being in low spirits affects you physically or whether the physical affects you spiritually. Either way, I have been decidedly 'out of sorts'. Sue Curley telephoned on Saturday and was really interested in the physical séance at Banbury. When I started to tell her of the Cockney lad Tim, who was circle leader from the Spirit side of life, she said, "Oh I know Tim, he used to come and keep me company when I was a taxi driver". Apparently he would sit in her passenger seat and chat. He loved staring out of the window. Some time ago a medium friend of her's informed her that Tim was 'very busy' being with Spirit, as 'a universal guide'. It sure is a small world even taking Spirit realms into account.

This morning (Monday, 20th December) I spoke to Dr Patel by telephone and after checking on my well being, diet etc. he said he would post me my third month's supply of Carctol. So we plod on despite how we feel! I did receive a great boost this morning when Val and Jan came here to give me healing. Jan brought with her her son Geoff, who is home from University. What a great lad, a real chip off the old block. Geoff is trained as a healer too and so I had the three of them working on me. I'm getting used to all this fuss, it seems the norm now. I felt much stronger and uplifted following this healing session, but I did comment that I couldn't sense Spirit around me for the last few days. I thought that perhaps it had been my request for them to step back for a few days to give me a rest. However, Jan and Val assured me that they were still very much there and before the close of today I was to receive some very humorous reassurance of this myself. I spent several hours today typing up my book on the computer. I went to 'shut down' and take my disc out, I blinked and looked again at the computer screen. The screen saver which Paul loaded months ago (way before this present saga) is a picture from Nick Parks' animation, 'The Wrong Trousers' (we are great fans of his in our home). The particular scene on this screen saver is the one where Penguin (here we go again) is lying back testing out Grommit's (the dog) bed instead of going into the guest room. So there is Penguin reclining with Grommit's framed picture of a bone over the bed head. There on the background of this simple little picture were several perfect little spirit faces, I even recognised a couple of them from the videos. One was the broad faced, long bearded Chinese man complete with scull cap as seen on the Jan Higgins healing video. Fearing, yet again, that I might be becoming fanciful I asked Steve to come and look and yes he saw them straight away. I am going to ask Paul if he could print this out a little larger than it is. Yet another piece of evidence for us, and what a humorous way of proving it - it certainly made me laugh, blooming penguins again eh!

I also chanced to take a second look at the internet print out which Val Snow had brought me of Doctor Joseph Bell who, if you remember, had come through to Jan Higgins in trance on Monday night. Yes, you've guessed it, there are tiny spirit faces on this computer print out too, again, some of them I recognise. Whatever next I wonder!

Well, I've managed to take a couple of days off my scribing but there are now a few developments on the 'spirit face' front to be reported. On Tuesday (21$^{st}$ December) Val phoned. She was in an excited state and reported that her husband, Ian, had been printing off some digital family photos on their computer. As they got them up on the screen circles of light began appearing as they watched. They showed themselves on the curtains, on clothes, in front of a bookcase and above head level. The colours were amazing and one circle contained a large eye in various shades of red. Val said she would print them off and bring them along to church on Wednesday evening.

Wednesday, 22 December 2004.

Steve accompanied me to our last service of the year. The place looked lovely in the candlelight and the committee had obviously 'worked their socks off'. Jean and Mike Kelford did a lovely service and it was great to see everyone again. Val brought her computer prints as promised and they were amazing, but according to Val, not as amazing as they are on the computer screen, so I've promised to call in for a peep at the originals. Her daughter is rather 'spooked' by these photos, but I really can't be blamed here can I? I wasn't even there when it happened. Paul also took a mobile phone photo when he was out with his friends at an old quarry this week and, yes, there were spirit faces and plenty of them. It's obviously not just a phenomenon which occurs in my presence but has now spread to those connected to my story.

Gerald Townsend-Howes videoed the service on Wednesday and I have brought it home to check it out for spirit, which I haven't done as yet.

Today is Christmas Eve and having watched my video of Alistair Simm as Scrooge I am now in the Christmas spirit! I spoke with our good friends Adrian and Liz Tucker – Peake this morning and was told, "Our house is your house", just come and go as you please tomorrow. That will be just dandy and greatly appreciated. In the afternoon I went up to have a rest and just as I had settled into bed I noticed a spirit face of a lady, quite a large one, staring across from the dark mahogany surface of our wardrobe. I always have to check now that I am not being fanciful and so called Paul in. I suggested we take a photo with his mobile and there was the lady. Steve came upstairs and immediately saw her too! Gosh, I'll be asking them to 'smile for the camera' next, won't I?
I have a feeling this lady may be my Nan because of the face shape and hairstyle but I can't be sure here.

Healthwise I do really feel that I am deteriorating now, feeling an increasing shortness of breath and aching in my limbs. My pallor is none too rosy now and I can do very little without becoming tired and how do I feel about the prospect of passing? Well it's a very mixed experience being in this situation and I will try to express it as honestly as possible. My main concern is leaving Steve and Paul, how will they be without me? Steve is spending practically every waking minute looking after me and the house. Paul has whizzed the vacuum around this morning and Steve is beginning to sound like me, asking what I will want for tea tomorrow and when I say I don't know, getting ratty with me and saying, jokingly, "You have to plan ahead with meals, Shirley" just like I used to say to him. He also gets irritated if I don't appear at the dining table within five seconds of being called, this used to annoy me beyond all measure too! It's like a role reversal and we can both see the funny side of it! But, seriously, I'm having to learn to let go of the tasks which I have done for the last seventeen years and it's not easy. Steve, very unselfishly, just wants me to rest and do the things I enjoy doing and most importantly to get my book completed.

As to how I feel about leaving everyone, well I can honestly say I'm not depressed or feeling sorry for myself. I am a little uneasy at the manner of it, none of us like pain do we? But as for the destination I am really excited. Even now thinking of waking up in another dimension minus pain and discomfort and meeting, again, my loved ones, well how could anyone not be looking forward to it in a way. I would obviously stay, given the choice, but the matter is out of my hands and what will be, will be. Death is probably even more wonderful than birth, it's only sad for those left behind. We have to look at the whole picture, the wider perspective and keep a balanced overview. Meanwhile, I shall do my best to enjoy what looks like might be my last earthly Christmas.

Christmas day was most enjoyable and very relaxing. I even managed to 'drop off' in an armchair during the afternoon. Adrian and Liz made us so welcome, as ever, and it was nice to spend the day with folks you feel so completely at home with. But today, Boxing day, I feel wretched, I am indescribably tired and my appetite is practically non-existent - to hell with the green lentils and Soya milk today! *(Shirley was on a strict Ayurvedic vegetarian diet on the advice of Dr Patel – Steve Bach)* I am wondering today if I will be able to stand the journey to Coventry on Wednesday for my initial radiotherapy appointment. There will be at least ten subsequent visits on consecutive days. I'll try and start the procedure off and see how I feel. I am getting quite considerable pain in the breast area now.

Val and Jan chatted at length today and Val's husband, Ian, feels that the 'spirit orbs' on their digital photos were caused by the light reflected from the lens of the camera. I explained to Val that, yes, of course it could be but that only means that Spirit World are using that light to show themselves. After all, as this happens, there has to be a logical scientific explanation for it. Man only uses the term 'magic' or 'miracle' to describe things currently beyond his knowledge. As these things do occur it is by the Spirit World using earthly matter, light etc. and mixing it with substance from their own plane of existence to create what they need to be able to show themselves to us. So what? If the reflection from a camera lens is used, Spirit is merely employing what is available to them like the previous orbs in church. Val's orbs all contain faces or eyes, the faces having obviously been added by spirit.

Today, 27th December, Mel informed me that her daughter Sara's partner, Manu, a consultant urologist, is trying to purchase Carctol. He has been making a study of the substance ever since my illness brought it to his attention. Apparently Carctol works by boosting the immune system particularly encouraging the 'T' cells which are our immune system's normal cancer fighters. Chemotherapy may kill cancer cells but is indiscriminate, destroying healthy cells also, together with invaluable 'T' cells. I am glad that Manu is so interested in Carctol. Even if I don't make it, my plight will have helped by bringing the product into the limelight. Manu reports that Carctol has just been registered as a drug as well as herbal medicine.

Well today, 29th December, was time for my trip to Coventry to be 'measured up' for radiotherapy. The journey wasn't too bad but then a lot of folk are still on their Christmas break so traffic was light. It took us fifty minutes. We were attended to promptly but the measuring process I found uncomfortable in the extreme. I had to lie flat on my back on a hard table-like contraption. This wouldn't have been so bad had it been just my breast that is bad, but the liver tumors now make it painful to lie flat out and getting myself back into a sitting position is a nightmare. It was also very uncomfortable having to put both arms back behind my head to grip a bar. In the end, they had to use a strap support for my bad side. Anyway, I'm now marked with small dots of permanent blue ink and hopefully the treatment itself will be quicker than this measure up.

I have just heard, two days later, that my first appointment is to be on the 12th January, quite a wait really, considering how rapidly the cancer is growing. I really wonder if I'll still be on planet Earth by the 12th January let alone well enough to travel to and from Coventry every day!

It's now New Year's Eve and this morning Jan Higgins and son Geoffrey came to give me healing. I feel much better for it and asked Jan how Spirit feels about my health at this stage. She replied, that they certainly haven't given up on me and are trying their method of de-materialising tumors. They make no promises regarding the outcome. Jan herself has been told that she should be working with Spirit on cancer patients and she is keen to collect some patients and try and help. Maybe Jan's healing work is the prime reason for my 'guinea pig' status. There are still endless possibilities. I observed that Jan looked a little pallid and tired this morning and she explained that she has been involved in much 'rescue work' for Spirit since the appalling Tsunami in South East Asia. Apparently poor lost souls have been coming to her, clairvoyantly, for help. They all lost their lives so suddenly and are now finding themselves with many of the people they were with on the Earth plane. Most of them do not realise that they have 'died'. They wander back to where their homes were only to find them gone. Jan had to explain their new situation to them and direct them to the light of Spirit so that they can start their new life. This was becoming so exhausting that now, as they arrive, she instructs them to wait exactly where they are and when there are enough of them she will return and help them all together. This seemed to be working, Jan said, and she now reckons to be advising batches of one thousand spirits at a time. Her guide, 'Sir', (who was, if you remember, of help to me at the beginning of this illness) apparently came through with a message last year warning of an enormous humanitarian disaster in Asia. He forecast a death toll of over 100,000 and said many people like Jan would have to help the poor souls concerned.

The Macmillan nurses telephoned today (4th January) and suggested it would be wise for me to be checked by my G.P. in case my breathlessness is due to retention of fluid. Dr Fernell arrived very promptly and felt that although heart and lungs were fine there may be some abdominal fluid retention and has prescribed a course of tablets. I told him that if I could hail a bus with 'Spirit World' on the front I would just step on and wave everyone "Au revoir". I added that I'd asked Steve if I could be 'put down' but he'd said "No" as it had cost twenty five pounds to have our hamster put out of it's misery! Dr Fernell smiled saying, "Oh don't do that, there's too much paper work involved". Tomorrow, Jenny, the Macmillan nurse, is paying her first visit.

# End Chapter

**I** have delayed the writing of this chapter because of not knowing how things will end for me. I have now reached such a decline in my health that, if I'm honest, I now feel it is my time to pass to spirit. I am not afraid, as there is not a doubt within me about the next life and how wonderful it is. I can hardly wait to see so many people over there, particularly Mom and Dad. This is definitely not to say that I wouldn't choose to stay if I could, but it's no use wishing, this is how things are and to kick against it would be a complete waste of emotional energy. I only hope I don't have too rough and painful a passage.

This book is my spiritual perspective. It is the view I have formed after many experiences of my own and from knowing many other spiritualists. I do not expect everyone to relate to all of it in its entirety, but if those who read it can each glean some benefit then my writing it has been worthwhile. It has been 'real hard graft' but I know that Spirit has helped and inspired me and I'm so glad I've managed before popping off to the next realm. If this book helps the cause of Spiritualism to move a little further towards its inevitable maturity then it will have done a good job.

In some ways a miraculous recovery would have been such a positive ending to all this. It would have been such a good advert for Carctol, spiritual healing or even psychic surgery. However, my trying all of these alternatives has been a very positive experience and my investigations along the way have proved that these methods have worked for many many people. Carctol, in particular, has a great track record so if ever you are unfortunate enough to be ill with cancer, give it a go!

Hope has been my companion along this journey and I still feel that all this was meant to be somehow. It is not always possible to see reasoning behind the Divine plan. It's strange but my friend and neighbour Mac, some months ago, gave me the words to the hymn "God moves in a mysterious way, his wonders to perform." It's strange that this should come my way because the way for me at the moment is indeed very mysterious. But then Jesus told us "In my father's house there are many mansions, if it were not so, I should have told you". We are building every day of our earthly life the place we will inhabit one day in the Spirit World. We can only pass to the level of spiritual vibration which we have earned through the way we have lived here. The implications of this are colossal. You may have been a regular churchgoer, chanting creeds and taking part in elaborate rituals but this will only have helped if it made you a kinder and better human being. Others may seldom, or indeed never, have set foot inside a church, but if they have lived a positive, unselfish spiritual life then their place in the after life will be a happy one. So, we cannot make vast generalisations, all men are equal but at different stages in their development. No man should dictate to another what he should think but it is always beneficial to share thoughts with one another. I hope that maybe a few people who read my book will go along to a spiritualist church out of curiosity. It may not be your 'cup of tea', but it could turn out to be your spiritual home, like it did for me!

I have wondered all through this illness not whether it came along for a reason but what that reason is. Was it to be a test for the herbal medicine Carctol or a test of psychic surgery or spiritual healing? Was it the manifestation of the dozens and dozens of spirit faces, firstly on video, then mobile phone screen and finally on computer printouts. I feel that these faces have certainly confirmed beliefs for some and caused others to open their eyes for the possibility of a spirit realm. Then again, maybe the prime motive was spurring me on to write a book. Perhaps I was always meant to do it. I feel also that it has been tied in with the development of healing, particularly with the work Jan Higgins is to do. I would suggest to everyone that it is wise to make your own search. Use your powers of thought and perception to fathom out what follows this life. Do not be content to blindly accept what others tell you (and that includes me). Forward thinking often makes you unpopular because the establishment always feels threatened by it. Copernicus, Darwin, Newton and Galileo were all charged with being religious, but now their brilliant forward thinking is accepted as a part of science. This is how the after life will one day be understood, history will merely be repeating itself by turning what was once scoffed at as 'magic' into tangible fully comprehended continuation of science.

For me, this earthly span is such a minute part of the whole that far from feeling I am approaching an end I know that a new horizon is dawning. I will do my utmost to be in touch with you all.

Always aim for one thing,
'That this earth will have been a better place from your journey through it'. It's as simple as that

Au revoir.

*Shirley.*

*Shirley left us on the afternoon of Friday, 14th January 2005 aged 47 years. It was a lovely, sunny afternoon.*
*She passed peacefully and gently, lying in her own bed at home, her favourite place, the sun shining through her window. She was with some of the people she was closest to and in the place she loved best.*

*Steve Bach*

# SHIRLEY'S DAILY AYERVEDIC MEDICINE

## *MORNING*
1 Evening Primrose capsule
1 Carctol capsule
1 Vasa tablet
1 Sitopaladi tablet
1 Karela tablet

## *LUNCHTIME*
1 Carctol capsule
1 small black pill

## *EVENING MEAL*
1 Carctol capsule
1 Vitamin B Complex tablet

## *BEDTIME*
1 Carctol capsule
1 Vasa tablet
1 Sitopaladi tablet
1 Karela tablet
1 small black pill

# Shirley's Speech*

Hello to all of you and welcome to this wonderful little church which is my spiritual home and has been for the last 11 years.

Although I am sad to leave you all please understand that I am only moving on. My earthly journey is done and a new exciting life is beginning. My discarded 'overcoat' is not here today. I didn't like the idea of that somehow and it's irrelevant now anyway. *I'm* here and that's what matters.

The last few months have been the most interesting and exciting of my life. This might sound bizarre to some of you but from discovering my illness to my last day was an adventure and along the way I met many wonderful folk. I came to realise how many great people have filled my life. I have been so lucky all along life's road and wouldn't change a thing. This has been the pathway of Shirley Anne Bach and was all meant to be.

Recently it has been difficult to share all the strange things which have happened to me as I realise not all of you are on 'the same wavelength' as me. But I know that everyone has tried to help and encourage according to his or her beliefs and with love in their hearts. I assure you that every card, flower and telephone call has been of great help to me, even if at times I hadn't the energy to respond to you. You really are a great bunch.

Of course, being me, I have to try to sow a few spiritual seeds here and give my forthcoming book 'a plug'. The initial idea was triggered by my consultant surgeon, Nick Purser, a lovely man and obviously of a really spiritual nature himself. As soon as the challenge was laid down I was 'like a dog with a bone' and although it's been hard work I've really enjoyed the process and feel I was destined to write it. Please appreciate that the chapters were written as my adventure unfolded and had no more idea than any of you how it was all to work out.

In some ways I'm sorry the ending has had to be sad. Firstly I would have liked to stay with you all and I feel that I had much more to give. Secondly a miraculous recovery would have inspired others and perhaps led them to try alternative therapies and spiritual healing. However I have always been sensible enough to know that once your allotted time has come nothing can alter this. I now have to set off on a great journey and am looking forward to being with loved ones on the other side. I have been up to now, like all of you, a little seedling in the nursery bed and now it's time for the 'great planting out'.

I know that one or two of you think that this earthly life is all that there is and I hope you will excuse my 'conceit' in telling you that you are wrong! So Robin and Clive** watch out, if I haunt anyone it will be you two; I'm out to prove it to you! I never thought I'd see you two here; it's amazing what lengths you have to go to sometimes.

The main positive thing to have come out of my illness is, without a doubt, the phenomenon of spirit faces are now showing themselves on video, computer and photos. This is a great leap forward for spiritualism and I hope they will help everyone to a greater understanding. One day, I believe, the existence of spirit will be incorporated into scientific understanding. We are well on track here and I hope I've helped in my little way.

Let us never forget in all this that the main ingredient of our earthly lives should be love. It matters not what religion you are, no one is better than anyone else and we all go to the next world regardless. As I've always said to my son Paul, never do anything to anyone else that you wouldn't want done to you. A simple philosophy but wouldn't it be a wonderful world if we all did that!

Don't worry too much about material things either as at the end of the day we leave it all behind us. We can only take with us the person that we are. Doing good with what we've got while we're here is the only way we can take our riches with us.

My message to all who run this church is 'keep up the good work'. This temple of healing and light is priceless. All do what you can to help; pull together for the cause. New blood is needed on committee as Mel and Sue have done their fair share. Don't hesitate to volunteer. I can assure you that, as with life itself, you will get far more out than you ever put in! I know I would have been lost without this place. I have every intention of still being a part of church life only now, of course, I'll be helping from a new perspective. It is important to me that life goes on in a positive manner for all of you especially Steve and Paul. I just know that you will look after them for me until we're all together again.

My love is with every single one of you and remember one day we'll all be reunited. There is no end just a moving on.

We are told from spiritual communications that our after-life conditions depend on how we have lived our earthly life. We can only go to the level of spiritual vibration to which our development befits us and we will accordingly dwell with others of a like spiritual outlook. This definitely deserves thinking about I think you'll agree. Anyway, I have done my best and we can't ask more of ourselves than that, can we.

Please sing your hearts out today. There's nothing worse than feeble singing at a funeral and don't forget to buy the book when it's published. All profit will go to the church funds.

Finally let's bear one last point in mind and ensure that this world is enriched in some way by our journey through it.

GOD BLESS

SHIRLEY

*Read by Alan Perry at the Celebration of Shirley's Life at Bromsgrove Spiritualist Church, Church Road, Catshill, Bromsgrove, Worcestershire on Friday 25th February, 2005.*

*\*\*Robin Goundry and Clive Brooks – wonderful friends who are very sceptical about any 'afterlife'.*

# Thankyou

During the compilation and production of this book I gratefully acknowledge the contributions made by the following:

Sue Detheridge and Mel Clark for their time spent typing, Margaret Green for assistance in proof reading, Olwyn Griffiths for the cover design, Jean Kelford for publishing advice.

There are many, many other people, some of whom are mentioned in this book, without whom our lives would have been much the poorer, especially near the end of Shirley's short life. My thank you goes out to you all for your support, love and care.

Steve Bach